THE COMPLETE BOOK OF
FLOWER ARRANGEMENT

The Complete Book

f Flower Arrangement

FOR HOME DECORATION
FOR SHOW COMPETITION

F. F. Rockwell
(EDITOR-IN-CHIEF, *THE HOME GARDEN*)

ad Esther C. Grayson

WITH 89 FULL-COLOR ILLUSTRATIONS
BY F. W. CASSEBEER
AND DRAWINGS
BY JOHN BURTON BRIMER

The American Garden Guild, Inc.
ad Doubleday & Company, Inc., 1954

PRINTED AT THE COUNTRY LIFE PRESS, GARDEN CITY, N.Y., U.S.A.

Dedicated to
those garden club members
the country over who have brought
the art of American Flower Arrangement
to its present high standard

Foreword

Despite predictions made many years ago that the art of flower arrangement would be but a temporary fad, soon forgotten, this new art is still with us; instead of receding, the interest in it continues to grow.

A dozen years have elapsed since our first book on Flower Arrangement appeared. The reception given this and a second volume published in 1940, and requests from many readers of *The Home Garden,* has resulted in the preparation of the present book, which we feel not only brings the subject up to date, but is much more comprehensive than its predecessors.

In writing *The Complete Book of Flower Arrangement* we fortunately have had available for illustrations Fredrick Cassebeer's unequaled collection of kodachromes of flower arrangements. We have been equally fortunate in having as an artist John Burton Brimer, whose agile pencil is quick to supplement written expositions and suggestions with drawings or sketches that graphically visualize the points under discussion.

We take this opportunity also to express our thanks to the noted flower artists who have co-operated by supplying several of the chapters on special types of arrangements: Barbara Beck, President of the Federated Garden Clubs of New York State, Inc.; Esther Wheeler; Anne Elizabeth Erhorn; Claire Stickles; Louise Hoffman, and Natalie Bowen; and to such organizations as the New York Federation of Garden Clubs, the Garden Club of America, the Garden Club of New Jersey, and the New York and Pennsylvania Horticultural societies. Most of the half-tone illustrations, from the cameras of Adrian Boutrelle, Charles R. Pearson, and Gottscho-Schleisner, have been made available through the courtesy of these sources.

F. F. ROCKWELL

ESTHER C. GRAYSON

GrayRock
August 1947

Contents

Contents

PART THREE

PLANT MATERIALS FOR ARRANGEMENTS

Part One

THE ART OF ARRANGEMENT

TAILORED TO FIT: This room—one of a series shown by The Garden Club of America at the International Flower Show in New York—illustrates how arrangements can be made to harmonize with their surroundings in the home.

CHAPTER I

Fun with Flowers

You don't have to be an expert at the game to have a lot of fun with the art of arranging flowers. Perhaps you've hesitated to try your hand at it, held back by the impression that it's all a great mystery, and that you couldn't expect to accomplish anything worth while until you had won your way to the inner circles of the cult. Forget it! Throw your fears out of the window and make up your mind to start in on your own.

Why should you make "arrangements" of flowers instead of merely sticking them haphazardly into a vase or a bowl the way Grandma used to do? She had surplus blooms from that famous hardy border of hers (in which everything seemed to grow to perfection without benefit of sprays, dusts, vitamin tablets, or California earthworms), and of course she used them in bouquets for indoor decoration, even though she'd never heard of "arrangements."

Perhaps you feel that what was good enough for Grandma is good enough for you. But the fact of the matter is that it's really a lot more fun to make arrangements with your flowers. With a little practice you'll find yourself putting them together in such a way that they will show off to much better advantage than if they were crowded together without any attempt at working out a design. And these arrangements will add much more to the decoration of your rooms than did the jammed-together bouquets of yesteryear. You'll get a deal of satisfaction, too, from the admiration your friends and guests will have for your increasing skill in so handling flowers that they become features of decorative schemes for rooms rather than just a part of the general surroundings that never receives—nor merits—a second look.

Too frequently the person who is contemplating starting in with flower arrangement gets off on the wrong foot by considering it solely, or at least primarily, a means of winning prizes or awards at flower shows. This is an unfortunate state of affairs, and one for which the garden clubs must admit their share of responsibility. Lectures on flower arrangement and courses in judging put disproportionate emphasis on the flower-show angle. Let exhibition arrangements point the way, display new materials, or new ways of utilizing old ones, set high standards in this recently developed western art; but let us never lose sight of the fact that flower arrangement, while admittedly an art, is one that belongs to and in the home.

Don't be afraid to make a start. Lack of experience did not deter you from your first attempts at growing flowers; do not let it keep you from trying to use them artistically after you have grown them. As a gardener you had to take the first plunge—and learn by making mistakes. Assume the same attitude toward arranging your flowers. Take it for granted that you will make mistakes and that the results of your first attempts will not be masterpieces. Probably you'll get a good laugh from some of them. But with practice you'll improve, and you'll have a lot of fun doing it. Things which were difficult at first—mechanical tricks in handling flowers and foliage, the selection of colors that do not clash, the use of containers that "go with" the plant materials you wish to place in them—will gradually become second nature. You'll soon find yourself *thinking* in terms of arrangement: an unusual flower or bit of foliage, a particularly pleasing combination of colors, a utensil that formerly you never would have thought of using as a vase—all these will suggest ideas for arrangements; and your attempts to work them out will prove an endless challenge and a source of pleasure.

You will find, too, that the more you learn about making arrangements of your own, the more you will be able to appreciate and enjoy those made by others. Your visits to flower shows will take on a new interest. You'll no longer be satisfied to say merely, "I like this," or, "I don't like that"; you'll know why one composition is satisfying and another is not. And this ability to analyze the work of others will in turn aid you immensely in improving your own.

Speaking of fun with flowers, one should not overlook a companion interest that to many has provided a fascinating hobby —the collection of containers to be used in making arrangements. Most of us have experienced, in mild or in acute form, the malady known as collector's itch. Often the objects of the collector's passion serve no useful purpose, but in this case they do. You may not care to carry this hobby as far as do several persons of our acquaintance who fill closets and shelves with "pieces," some of which are certainly God-awful junk; but the gradual acquisition of a dozen or two well-selected vases, bowls, and other suitable receptacles will provide an intriguing pursuit. A friend of ours on Cape Cod has specialized in miniature containers and grows all sorts of miniature flowers to put into them. Every morning during summer and fall she amuses herself with making a number of tiny arrangements to decorate various tables, shelves, and window sills. She has learned how to have fun—lots of it—with her flowers.

Arrangements in the Home

And while we're talking about having more fun with your flowers by learning to make real arrangements with them let's discuss for a moment another phase of the subject before we plunge into the technique of making arrangements. Never for a moment should we lose sight of the fact that the arrangement is a means to an end rather than an end in itself. *The purpose*

5

of the art of flower arrangement is to contribute an additional note of cheerfulness and happiness to our home surroundings.

The first step in the effective use of arrangements is to realize that each vase or bouquet, pleasing though it may be in itself, is but one of many factors that contribute to the general effect. The flower arrangement, when placed in a room, becomes a part of a larger composition.

If both the arrangement and the background and surroundings are appropriate to one another, then the decorative effect of each is enhanced. If, on the contrary, either one is not appropriate to the other, they will greatly detract from each other.

The principles that should be followed in connection with making flower arrangements apply equally to the placement of an arrangement in a room. Design, scale, balance, and harmony must all be kept in mind if the best effects are to be achieved.

In other words, the arrangement should so fit into its surroundings as to form part of the over-all *design;* it should be neither too large nor too small for the position it is to occupy *(scale);* it should be placed in such relation to other objects back of and around it that it becomes part of the picture, not a disturbing element *(balance);* and in character and color it should be congenial with the character of its surroundings *(harmony).*

To take a few extreme cases by way of illustration, a miniature arrangement placed on a grand piano would look rather ludicrous because so patently out of scale; a nice, fat mass arrangement at one end of a mantel with ornaments grouped symmetrically on it, and a picture over the center, would be obviously out of balance; and an Orchid piece in a kitchen window would not be in harmony with its surroundings.

The Chinese have an old saying that one picture tells more than a thousand words. If you'll take the trouble to study carefully John Brimer's sketches (pages 60 and 84), we're sure you can get a clearer mental picture of the point being stressed than would be possible from text alone.

CHAPTER II

Past and Present

This is a "how to" manual on the arrangement of flowers in the present mode, and as such is little concerned with the history of the art. Nevertheless a very brief outline of what has gone before, of some of the influences that have been at work in one way or another to bring about the result which we know as Modern Flower Arrangement, serves the practical purpose of enabling the beginner to get a clearer picture of what it is all about.

In Western civilization flower arrangement is a comparatively recent art; in the Orient it goes back many hundreds of years.

In another respect, too, the Oriental and Occidental schools of flower arrangement have differed from each other, in fact have been almost diametrically opposed. In the former the plant material has been meager and the emphasis has been upon line design—to such an extent that, in Japan (where the art of flower arrangement has reached a higher degree of perfection than anywhere else in the world), such compositions of plant material form sharply etched silhouettes, with color of very secondary importance. In Japan, the art of flower arrangement has, for centuries, been given a place in public esteem on a level with the fine arts. In addition to that it has had deeply religious and social significance.

In China, floral decorations were used in connection with religious rites in the temples of Buddha; and when Buddhism

Arrangement by Mrs. Samuel F. Newkirk

An excellent example of modern mass arrangement, in which many flowers are used, but without the over-crowding characteristic of the early days of flower arrangement, and with careful attention to design.

Arrangement by Mrs. Nelson B. Grove

*In modern line arrangements emphasis on bold sil-
houette (characteristic of Japanese school) is retained,
but flowers and foliage are lavishly employed.*

spread to Japan this use of flowers went with it, took root, and has been assiduously cultivated ever since. Even as far back as the seventeenth century the Japanese were holding competitive exhibitions in the art of flower arrangement. With the passing of time many different "schools" developed and sought to gain converts to their own particular conceptions.

Gradually the rules developed by these schools became more and more rigid—just as most religious rituals, through repeated use and tradition, tend to crystallize. A slavish adherence to these rules has naturally resulted in fixed forms which, no matter how perfect in design and how beautiful in themselves, offer very little latitude for originality and personal creative expression.

Occidental Arrangement

Leaving for the moment the Oriental type of flower arrangement (it is presented up in more detail in Chapter XII), let us take a look at the beginnings of flower art in Western civilization.

In the West the first gardens were those planted and tended by the members of religious orders. While their fellowmen were engaged in war and conquest, trade and travel, the men of peace and good will devoted much of their time to the collecting and cultivating of herbs for cooking and healing, fruits for their meagerly set tables and their wine cellars, and flowers for decoration and religious ceremonies. In the West, however, flower arrangement never became an integral part of religious ceremonies, nor gained any particular religious significance; and has remained almost completely devoid of any such connotation, even though flowers are frequently used as church and altar decorations.

It is in old flower paintings—dating back to 1700 or thereabouts—that we have our best records of what we may consider the beginnings of real art in the arrangement of flowers in Europe and England (see pages 166 and 167). In all of

*Arrangements by Mrs. Loren R. Dodson (left) and Mrs. Tom
Cummings at Judges Course, N. Y. Federation of Garden Clubs*

*PAST AND PRESENT: Above are a mass arrangement
of the old-fashioned or period type and a Japanese line
arrangement; below, their contemporary counterparts, a
modern mass and a modern line arrangement.*

Mrs. William Joy   *Mrs. Anne Elizabeth Erhorn*

these old paintings there is evident at a glance the essential difference between what the Orientals considered art in the arrangement of flowers and the Occidental conception of it. They show, without exception, the lavish use of material of many species in compositions which, though they take up several times as much space as the average Oriental arrangement, are crowded almost to the limit of the last flower that can be stuck into the container. Also—in direct contrast to the Oriental arrangement—they are as lavish in the use and the range of color as they are of plant material.

What are known as "period" arrangements are merely the several types or styles of mass arrangements which developed in different countries or eras. Unlike the Japanese schools of arrangement, however, they did not grow up side by side, nor were they based on any fixed rules of design, but on the general principles which apply to any artistic composition whether created with plant material or with pigments on a piece of canvas.

The differences between these various types of period arrangements do not exactly concern us here. As might be expected, Victorian arrangements were solid masses, rich in coloring, in keeping with the furniture and the décor of the day; the French Empire compositions, with more attention given to classic tradition, were less massive and executed with a lighter, more airy touch, and in gay and more delicate colors; Flemish and Dutch compositions were, if possible, even more solid than the Victorian; and if the paintings of the time represent them accurately, as they probably do, were supplemented by birds' nests, butterflies, bees, vegetables—"everything but the kitchen sink"; Colonial arrangements, made up of such simple flowers as graced Colonial gardens, and supplemented by grasses or weeds, were lacking in the finished elegance that characterized their European counterparts. Like the latter,

MODERN LINE: A few yellow Roses with Magnolia leaves. Arrangement by Mrs. Tom Cummings.

however, they were essentially mass arrangements and as such entirely distinct from the line compositions of the Orientals.

Modern Flower Arrangement

The type of flower arrangement which may justly be defined as "modern" is a hybrid resulting directly from the crossing of the severely stylized line arrangements of the East and the unfettered, robust, colorful arrangements of the West. In them are manifest some of the characteristics of both types; and they tend to possess, as many hybrids do, infinitely more vigor than either parent. (A study of the photographs shown on page 11 will illustrate this point.)

This modern flower arrangement is distinctly an American form of the art. It has been, and is still being, developed here. So far it has apparently had little effect abroad, although it has created some interest in England. This is, however, from what one hears, more a matter of curiosity than of emulation.

Undoubtedly the featuring of highly competitive classes in flower shows throughout the United States has been the most important factor in developing the American type of flower arrangement. In the beginning it was, quite naturally, an imitative art, a more or less abortive attempt at copying either the Japanese or the European examples of flower arrangement. Fortunately for the future of flower arrangement in this country, a few real artists became interested in the subject. Foremost among these was John Taylor Arms, president of the American Society of Etchers. His work in helping to judge arrangements at flower shows, and more particularly his many lectures to groups interested in the subject, resulted in breaking the shackles in which it found itself fettered and in giving it a vigorous start in the right direction.

MODERN MASS: Yellow Roses and Begonia leaves. Arrangement by Mrs. Albert R. Benedict.

American flower arrangement of the present day stands on its own feet. Acknowledging freely what it owes to the past, it nevertheless boldly establishes its own standards and, above all, encourages originality in both design and technique. These standards, of course, are not always lived up to. Flower arrangement is peculiarly an art for amateurs. As such it has a wide appeal to all who love flowers, whether they are so fortunate as to be able to grow their own, or depend upon the offerings of the flower shops.

Such "professional" arrangers of flowers as the commercial florists were at first inclined to scoff at the efforts of the amateurs, but little by little the new art has begun to affect even the unimaginative professionals in shops and the creations of the head gardeners on private estates in those increasingly rare instances where the preparation of floral decorations is still left in their hands. More and more frequently one sees passable or even good flower arrangements in florist-shop windows, and more and more they are being used as display pieces in the windows of stores of various sorts.

Flower Arrangement in the Home

In the average American home of today flower arrangement has an established place in the scheme of interior decoration. Walls are frequently finished in a single tone, or are paneled, and such neutral backgrounds form the best setting for a display of cut flowers. Women who have not the time, the inclination, or the specialized knowledge to do competitive exhibition work inform themselves on the principles of flower arrangement and practice it daily in their homes. In summer the cutting garden is a planned part of the landscaping, to provide a plenitude of flowers for the house at all times without robbing the beds and borders. In winter, a weekly visit to the florist is made as religiously as that to the grocer or butcher. We are flower-conscious in the best sense of the word, and see to it that there are always fresh, well-arranged blooms about us.

CHAPTER III

What Makes an Arrangement?

The first step toward being able to make flower arrangements of your own is to learn what constitutes an "arrangement" as that term is used in connection with flower-show exhibits and with similar compositions made up of flowers and foliage for home decoration.

It is by no means easy to give an exact definition. Many mere bouquets of flowers, which make no pretense at all of possessing any planned design, are attractive because of their charming colors or for the sheer beauty of the individual blooms of which they are composed.

Where, then, are we to draw a line? Where does a bunch or a bouquet of flowers cease to be merely that and become an "arrangement"?

To make a start in the direction of answering this question, let's simplify it by saying that an arrangement is a *composition,* whereas a bunch or a bouquet of flowers is not.

As a composition, our arrangement of flowers is subject to certain general principles or rules that apply to any composition in any medium—to a painting, an etching, a piece of sculpture, or an etude.

Even the arrangement of the furniture in the room in which you sit, if it is well done, forms a "composition" which complies with these same general principles. In using flowers for room decoration you will soon learn that, for satisfactory results, there must be a suitable relationship between the character of the arrangement itself and its surroundings—in other words, it becomes *a composition within a composition.*

The Basic Four Principles

Let us take a look at those general principles which apply to making a composition.

We'll start with the four principles that are perhaps most readily grasped: *Design, Scale, Balance,* and *Harmony.* There are others—which we will discuss later—but they are in the nature of further refinements of these basic four.

DESIGN is the form or shape of the composition—the thought-out plan upon which it is built. Take a look at any of the arrangements reproduced in this book. The one thing that must strongly impress you is that none of them could have "just happened." There is a *planned* relationship between all of the component parts; between the various flowers, the flowers and the foliage; between both of these and the particular container which holds them.

Design can be good, bad, or indifferent—but it is still design. A design that strikes one observer as being good may not appeal to another. To the admirer of "modern" art, for instance, the design in a composition by Dali or Picasso may seem the acme of perfection; whereas to one who admires such works as those of Corot or Bonheur it may seem the exact opposite. But the observer of either type of composition would still admit that it possesses design.

Arrangement by Mrs. Tom Cummings

DESIGN: *No matter how simple or how elaborate, a flower arrangement, to be worthy the name, must have perceptible design. Here Mrs. Cummings has achieved originality by ignoring the old-time rule that only uneven numbers of large blooms or leaves should be used.*

SCALE: the size-relationship of the component parts in a composition. Even to the untrained eye something seems wrong in the arrangement at the left. The fault lies in the use of such small and delicate flowers and foliage as Lily-of-the-valley and Fern fronds to support the large, bold forms of the Calla blooms. The container, too, is out of scale. Now note what happens when larger foliage and a larger container are substituted to bring the arrangement into better scale, as demonstrated at the right.

SCALE is the term used to denote the *size relationship* of the component parts of a composition. If, for instance, the "composition" happened to be a small living room, fitted with moderate-size pieces of furniture, a concert grand piano in one

Arrangement by Mrs. H. T. Langworthy

> *SCALE: From the first conception of an arrangement that is to be made, until the last flower or leaf is added, scale should be kept in mind. Especially important is the over-all size of the flower and foliage design in relation to the container. The arrangement above is an example of perfect scale in this respect.*

corner would be out of scale. Or the composition may be so simple a thing as a two-hundred-pound woman walking down the street, her head topped with a chic little chapeau about the size of a tomato can. You laugh—probably without realizing that the cause of your amusement is the violation of your intuitive sense of scale.

In a flower arrangement *scale* is achieved by selecting materials (flowers, foliage, or sprays) which in size are reasonably related to each other and to the container which holds them. A Calla-lily placed in the same vase with Spring Beauties or Lily-of-the-valley would be so obviously out of scale that even one who had never heard of flower arrangement would not think of using them together. This, of course, would be an extreme case, but it points the principle.

BALANCE may be somewhat more difficult for the beginner to grasp. But a little study of the arrangements shown on pages 23, 25, and 117, and of the sketches on page 24, should help make it plain. In a word, *balance,* in a flower arrangement (or in any composition in the graphic arts for that matter), is such a relationship of the component parts that it creates the impression of being stable—not inclined to tip either to the left or to the right. In a painting, or in the decoration of a room, balance is a *visual* impression only; in a flower arrangement, balance is even more noticeable; if balance is lacking, there is the feeling that the composition may actually tip over.

Balance is of two types—*symmetrical* and *asymmetrical.* In composing a flower arrangement, symmetrical balance is attained by making both "sides" of the arrangement practically

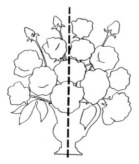
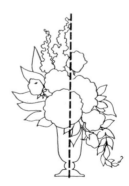

Arrangement by Mrs. Claire Stickles

BALANCE: It requires a nice artistic sense to achieve such an out-of-the-ordinary example of good balance as that attained here. The secret lies in the position of the plant material in relation to the container.

23

BALANCE: the arrangement of the component parts of a composition, in relation to each other, in such a way that the resulting "picture" has stability. Balance may be either symmetrical or asymmetrical, but there should be no feeling of a danger of "tipping over." Changing the position of the flowers above (left) results in greatly improved balance. Keeping large or dark-colored flowers low down in an arrangement helps achieve good balance, as does also a low or a dark container.

the same. (See line cut page 22.) In an asymmetrical arrangement the two sides (as separated by an imaginary line drawn down through the center) are distinctly different, but they have equal *weight*, and hence balance each other.

To a gardener these two types of "balance" are not new. He has employed both in laying out his grounds: symmetrical balance when he plants identical or matched groups of evergreens at either side of his door; asymmetrical when he has balanced a tall evergreen or shrub on one side of a gate or an arbor with a group of smaller specimens on the other.

HARMONY, the fourth principle, is a little more difficult to define because here we are dealing with intangibles, with aesthetic qualities rather than with physical properties. We can,

BALANCE

Any good arrangement
must possess balance. Most
easily achieved is symmetrical balance, such as that
shown above. But usually
asymmetrical balance (as
in the arrangement at
right) makes a more interesting design.

25

HARMONY: the aesthetic value in a composition resulting when the component parts supplement each other, with no discordant note. In the two arrangements above the design *is essentially the same, but summer-blooming Gladioli, combined with Forsythia and Crocus, are (to any gardener at least!) distinctly incongruous. When Daffodils are substituted, we get a more pleasing effect. Harmony in the use of* colors *is particularly important.*

perhaps, make a beginning by drawing some comparisons with other arts.

You know that when you look at a painting, or a building, or listen to a musical composition, it may give you a sensation of being pleasing, "all in tune"; or there may be somewhere a jarring note, a discord—in a word, lack of harmony. In a painting it may be one color that "fights" the others; in music a sour note. An elaborate colonial doorway on a tiny seaside cottage would at once strike you as being inharmonious.

Thus, in your flower arrangement, the several materials used and the container should be in harmony with one another. There should be no jarring note in scale, in color, or in character. Orchids and wild Violets arranged together, for instance, would probably do something to your stomach. Less violent discords might not be so obvious, but still you would recognize that something was wrong—that a lack of harmony existed.

Make a Start

With these few basic principles understood, you have sufficient information to make an intelligent start at arranging
flowers. Don't be too ambitious in your first attempts. The
simpler you keep them, the more clearly you will see how *design, scale, balance,* and *harmony,* if kept in mind while you
work, will influence and improve your results.

SUGGESTED EXERCISES. To make a beginning in this interesting art, suppose you look over such containers as are at hand
—vase, bowl, glass dish, or what-have-you—and gather a few
of such flowers as may be available. Then try to make an
arrangement similar to any of those illustrated—including the
"single-flower" arrangements on pages 13 and 134.

You will not find it so easy as it may at first appear. If you
think that flowers are perverse in the garden, you will find that
they can be even more so when you attempt to make them be-
have in an arrangement. But the challenge will intrigue you.

Nine Principles of Flower Arranging

Designedly, in the first part of this chapter, we have discussed but four of the many principles that apply to the making
of a really good flower arrangement. Our purpose in this was
to avoid giving the beginner so many things to think about at
one time that the result would be hopeless confusion. Having
now obtained an insight into some of the more important considerations to be kept in mind, we are ready to proceed a step
further, and to discuss these principles, and others, in more detail.

Your small boy who wants to take the alarm clock apart to
see what makes it tick may at times be annoying, but he has
the right idea. To see what makes a good arrangement we
must take one, or several, apart.

The "parts" of an arrangement, however, are not definite
mechanical entities, like the gearwheels and springs of an alarm
clock. No two arrangements are ever exactly alike, *but all good*

FOCUS: the bull's-eye or center of attention in a composition resulting from so placing the component parts that the eye is led to a central focal point. In a flower arrangement this is usually just above the container, often breaking the horizontal line of the top. In the arrangement above the four Dahlias of equal size not only distract the eye but leave an empty space where the focal point should be. Compare this lack of attention value with the improved focus of the arrangement at the right.

arrangements do have certain definite characteristics in common. By analyzing a number of arrangements we can reduce these characteristics to nine important principles.

These nine are: Design, Scale, Balance, Harmony, Focus, Rhythm, Accent, Repetition, and Unity. Because these principles (with the possible exception of Design) can be better il-

Arrangement by Mrs. J. C. Graham

FOCAL POINT: There are many ways of getting a center of interest in a flower arrangement. Here, of course, it is the two large Roses placed just above the rim of the container, emphasized by the stems of Grape-hyacinth, Lily-of-the-valley, and Glory-of-the-snow running into the center.

lustrated by graphic examples than by text, we have so treated them in the sketches shown on pages 20 to 36.

Some of these are more important than others; that is, their correct use, or their incorrect use or absence, in an arrangement

RHYTHM: the feeling of "swing" or motion in a composition, resulting from so arranging the main lines of the design that the eye is carried along them to, or through, the focal point. Study the two arrangements above and notice how one seems static, motionless, and the other suggests motion. These main lines should be determined before the arrangement is "filled in." In the arrangements above, plant material carries out the same sort of rhythm that is present in the design of the container.

will be more conspicuous in the case of some than of others. But all have their place.

Design, as has already been pointed out, is the form or shape of the composition (or arrangement) as a whole—the thought-out plan on which it is built. Design, of course, has dimensions. In a painting, or in a photographic reproduction of a flower arrangement, there are two—height and breadth. In an actual arrangement of flowers there is a third dimension—depth, from front to back.

In planning an arrangement—that is, in creating in your own mind a mental picture of the form it is to assume—these dimensions are the first things to consider. If it is an arrangement for a flower show, where each arrangement is usually placed in a "niche," you are given definite dimensions to start with.

*Arrangement at left by Mrs.
Anne Elizabeth Erhorn; below
by Mrs. Roderick R. Black*

S C A L E

and

R H Y T H M

*Scale involves a keen
sense of proportion as to
flowers and foliage, con-
tainer, accessory, base,
and background.
Rhythm, providing life
and added interest, is
achieved with graceful,
flowing lines.*

ACCENT: emphasis obtained for some particular area in the composition by giving it especial prominence. In a painting or photograph this may be done with high lights and shadows. In flower arrangements accent is usually accomplished by sharp contrasts (in color, size, or form) of some parts of the material used. Accent, properly employed, adds interest to the composition. The change to three dark flowers (above) does this, and also improves the balance and focus of the arrangement.

If it is to be a flower-show arrangement for a table or a window sill, or one for some particular place in your own living room, the dimensions will be less definite, but nevertheless they will be the factor that must be given first consideration when you start to plan the general design of your arrangement.

While any flower arrangement actually has three dimensions, most arrangements (probably nine out of ten, made

WHAT MAKES AN ARRANGEMENT? This beautiful composition of the foliage and flowers of Echeveria well illustrates the difference between a real arrangement and a bouquet. It was done for a class that called for "flowers in a metal container, stressing textural qualities." Check it with the principles of flower-arrangement art discussed in this chapter.

Arrangement by Mrs. Anne Elizabeth Erhorn at New York Judges Course

REPETITION: *repeating, in the composition, one or more ele-*
ments, such as forms or colors. Repetition is another method of
achieving accent. However, where it becomes too obvious, it defeats
its own purpose—just as a strained-for use of "apt alliteration's art-
ful aid" does in prose or poetry. A minor detail, "picked up" and
repeated, is magnified in effectiveness. Note accent value when more
cones are used. The black base also adds to the cumulative effect of
the several dark cones.

either for the home or for a show) will be viewed mainly from
one direction, and therefore are constructed largely on a two-
dimensional basis—width and height. The third dimension,
however, must not be lost sight of, for even an arrangement on
a mantel or against a wall will be seen at a slight angle from
the sides as well as from directly in front. The first problem,
however, is to learn to make an arrangement which will be
good even when viewed from a front position only. This is the
point that most concerns us right now.

First Steps in Analysis

If you have followed the suggestions already given and have
tried to make an arrangement like any of those shown, you
have probably discovered (as we warned you) that it wasn't

Arrangement by Mrs. Otho E. Lane

The effective use of color in an arrangement is not merely a matter of selecting harmonious hues, tones, or tints. The distribution of the color in the design, both in position and in area, is equally important. Here the design of the arrangement depends largely upon the way the color has been distributed.

so easy as it may have looked. If you will study John Brimer's sketches, you will understand more clearly what mistakes to look for in any arrangement, whether it be your own or another's. As a result you will find yourself automatically checking your own work, every time you make an arrangement, to

UNITY: *difficult to define, but it may perhaps be stated as the fitting-togetherness of all the elements which go to make up a composition. Unity includes Scale and Harmony, but is something more; it takes in the impression, the atmosphere, which the composition creates. In the arrangements of dried material depicted above the use of cut flowers (left) is out of character, a violation of unity. Texture, as well as form and color, is an important factor in achieving the impression of genuine unity.*

see if you are adhering to the principles that go into the making of a good composition—Design, Scale, Balance, Harmony, Focus, Rhythm, Accent, Repetition, and Unity.

One at a Time

If you attempt to analyze, or "take apart" any good arrangement (such as that on page 33, for instance), you can readily discern that it conforms to the four *basic* principles we have discussed: Design, Scale, Balance, and Harmony.

It is difficult, however, to follow in one arrangement all the principles that apply to the formation of a good composition, and for that reason we have singled them out one by one for illustration. In each of these sketches is shown not only the principle involved, but also an example of what happens if it is ignored. We suggest that, in studying these sketches, you at

first cover up, with a postcard or a piece of cardboard, the one at the right in each pair. (Perhaps unfortunately for this purpose the Brimer sense of good composition is so strong that even his "horrible examples" manage to look pretty attractive!)

SUGGESTED EXERCISES. We learn best *by doing*. Therefore the beginner at this intriguing art is urged, after reading these pages, to get together three or four "containers" (to the uninitiated, these are vases, pitchers, bowls, or what-have-you, that will hold flowers) and also a general assortment of cut flowers and foliage sprays, and then to experiment with each of the eight general principles illustrated by the series of drawings.

After trying out each principle by itself, he may attempt one arrangement, somewhat more elaborate, and then check it to see if it conforms to *all* the general principles of composition that have been discussed.

(NOTE: The reader who is a rank beginner, and who has never before tried making arrangements, will find it helpful to read Chapter VII, dealing with the mechanics of flower arrangement, before attempting the exercises suggested above. The information there given will save him a lot of experimenting in trying to get blossoms and foliage to "stay put" in the positions he would like them to assume.)

Arrangement by Mrs. Leon C. Forgie

FREE-FOR-ALL: The polychromatic or many-colored arrangement is seldom used in flower shows but is cheerful and gay for home decoration. In the example above the distribution of color gives emphasis to the form-design of the plant material.

CHAPTER IV

And Now We Come to Color

Up to this point we have discussed those principles of composition that have to do with *form* in the composition— design, scale, balance, focal point, and so on. Now we come to color, which, through all our discussion, has been fluttering around in the background like butterflies over a Buddleia bush. You can't very well divorce flowers from color.

Color is that fourth dimension that adds life, zip, and breath-taking dramatic quality to a good arrangement. It is so important that, when well handled, it often outbalances many another shortcoming in an arrangement, even to the extent of swaying the decisions of judges in the direction of a blue-ribbon award.

There are two sound reasons why any discussion of color has been delayed until this point. First, it is easier for the beginner to get a conception, in black and white, of the principles of composition and design without the added complications which color brings in. Second, any discussion of color, to be helpful, must be based upon some knowledge of what color *is*.

To the beginner no phase of the art of flower arrangement seems so complicated as that of the use of color, as it is ordinarily presented. Even the terms employed by writers and lecturers in discussing color are by no means standardized or uniform; and many a dissertation on the subject merely leaves the novice in confusion worse confounded.

We will attempt, then, to go into the subject of color with

sufficient thoroughness to give the beginner, in readily understood terms, at least the A B C of a working knowledge of it.

The Theory of Color

To imply that any adequate discussion of color could be
given in a single chapter in a book would indeed be presump-

THE "VOCABULARY" OF COLOR

THE SPECTRUM

*The straight band across the top of the opposite page is a re-
production of the* solar spectrum, *obtained by passing a ray of
sunlight through a prism. This gives a series of pure colors, or
"hues," ranging from red at one end to violet at the other, with
orange, yellow, green, and blue in between.*

THE COLOR CIRCLE

*When the hues of the spectrum—or others approximating
them—are arranged in the form of a ring, we have a color circle.
(See the middle one of the three concentric rings shown opposite.) The number of pure colors, or hues, varies with different
color "systems"; here there are six—red, orange, yellow, green,
blue, violet. These are termed* primary *hues. The divisions in between—such as violet-red, orange-red—are termed* secondary
hues.

SHADES, TINTS, AND TONES

*The addition of black, white, or gray (a combination of black
and white) to any of these hues will produce a new color. Black
produces a* shade; *white a* tint, *and gray a* tone. *The amount of
black, white, or gray determines the variations. Thus, in the
band at the* bottom *of the opposite page, black and white added
to orange-red give, respectively, progressive shades and tints of
this hue.*

COLOR HARMONIES

Certain combinations of color form "harmonies." A monochromatic *harmony consists of shades, tints, and tones of the
same hue; an* analogous *harmony, colors adjacent to each other
on the circle (such as violet, red-violet, and blue-violet); a* complementary *harmony, colors opposite each other (orange and
blue). Of the complementary harmonies several types are described in this chapter.*

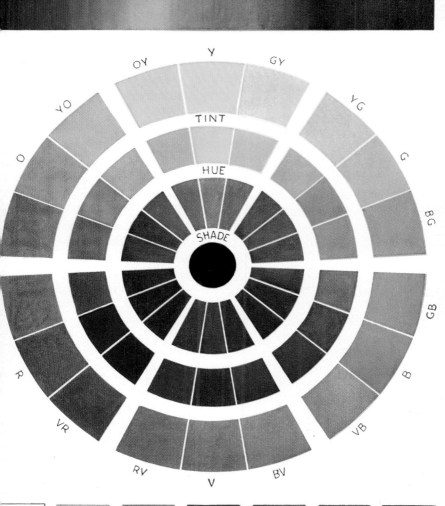

TINT

HUE

SHADE

OY Y GY

YO YG

O G

R BG

VR GB

RV B

V BV VB

tuous. But we can, perhaps, put the reader on a speaking acquaintance with it. So here is at least a nutshellful of information about it.

First of all, color, like sound, is the result of stimuli from outside transmitted to the brain through a specialized organ of the body. This organ, in the case of sound, is the ear; with color, the eye. The various "colors" of which we speak do not have separate *physical* identities in the sense in which we ordinarily think of them. They are the results of varying "light rays," just as the different notes in a musical scale are the result of sound waves.

If you require any demonstration of the fact that "colors" need have no physical embodiment, take a piece of white paper and a glass prism. Then hold the latter so that it catches a ray of direct sunlight. The white ray of sunlight, passing through the prism, is spread out upon the white paper as a multicolored band, with red at one end and violet at the other.

Where do these colors come from?

They appear because each light ray producing them (all bound up together in the ray of "white" sunshine) has its own angle of refraction, and is bent accordingly as it passes through the prism. The multicolored band that results (see top of page 41) is known as the solar spectrum and forms the basis of the definition of the various colors we know as red, green, blue, et cetera.

Now let's take our spectrum and bend it around into a circle with the ends touching—like a serpent swallowing its own tail. Then we have the "color circle," the mystic symbol of which flower arrangers prate so much. But the colors aren't marked off into neat little sections; they run together or blend. For purposes of discussion we cut the circle up into segments. Different authorities do this in different ways. One of the most practical for the beginner is the eighteen-segment circle, with six primary colors (or, more accurately, "hues")—Red, Orange, Yellow, Green, Blue, and Violet; and with twelve secondary or intermediate hues—violet-red, orange-red, red-orange, yellow-orange, orange-yellow, et cetera.

This arrangement of hues and intermediate hues is shown in the *center* ring of the three in the circle on page 41.

Shades, Tints, and Tones

So far, so good. We have taken a first step toward arriving at a basis for discussing color. But at once we run into another problem, for there are hundreds of colors other than those we find in traveling around the color circle. What about them?

Let us go back to the solar spectrum on the sheet of white paper. The paper *is* white because it is of a substance that *reflects* all of the many light waves combined in the ray of sunlight. If we substitute a paper that *absorbs* all the light waves —a *black* paper—then the spectrum disappears altogether. White is a combination of all colors; black (though usually spoken of as a color) is the absence of all colors.

Now if we take any one of the hues on the color circle and add black to it, we get a "shade" of the same color. If we add white, we get a "tint." If we add gray (which is a mixture of black and white), we get a "tone." But in each case it is still the same hue. To recapitulate:

Adding black produces a *shade*.
Adding white produces a *tint*.
Adding gray produces a *tone*.

To get a visual demonstration of these differences, study carefully the "Color Triangle" on page 45. Here a single hue (jade), at the apex of the triangle is changed, in three directions, by the additions of black, white, and gray, producing the series of shades, tints, and tones shown. Any combination of these associated or sub-colors forms a *monochrome*. This color triangle is reproduced from *The American Colorist* by Faber Birren, a leading authority on the subject of color.

Color Harmonies

What has all this got to do with arranging flowers?

From a practical point of view, so far as your own arrangements are concerned, it may mean little or it may mean much. For most persons certain combinations of color seem to "go together"—to harmonize. Other combinations "scream at each other"—are discordant. How can we tell which combinations are harmonious and which are not? Are there any rules to be followed? Rules in plenty have been laid down, but you will get far more help from a few basic principles. As is the case with design, so in employing color, no set of rules can assure success. There are guiding principles, but before these can be stated we need more definitions.

Complementary colors are those which lie directly *opposite* each other on the color circle; as, for instance, orange and blue; yellow and violet; red and green. Such "opposite" colors, when combined, produce neutral gray.

Analogous colors are those which lie *adjacent* to each other on the color circle—orange and red; blue and green; or a primary color, such as yellow, with orange-yellow and green-yellow.

Return now to the color harmonies we would like to get in our flower arrangements. These, in general, are of two types: groups of colors which are harmonious because they are like each other—that is, closely associated on the color circle; and groups of colors which directly contrast with each other—opposites on the color circle.

A *monochromatic harmony* is one in which the colors used are of the same hue, supplemented by shades, tints, or tones of the same hue.

An *analogous harmony* is one in which the colors used are those which adjoin each other on the color circle.

A *complementary harmony* is one in which they are direct, or nearly direct, contrasts. Of these there are four types: *direct complements; "split" complements,* in which one hue is used not with its direct complement, but with hues on either side of that complement—such as orange with green-blue and violet-blue; *triads,* combinations of three hues, equidistant from each other around the circle—such as orange, green, and violet; and *tetrads,* employing four hues spaced equidistantly.

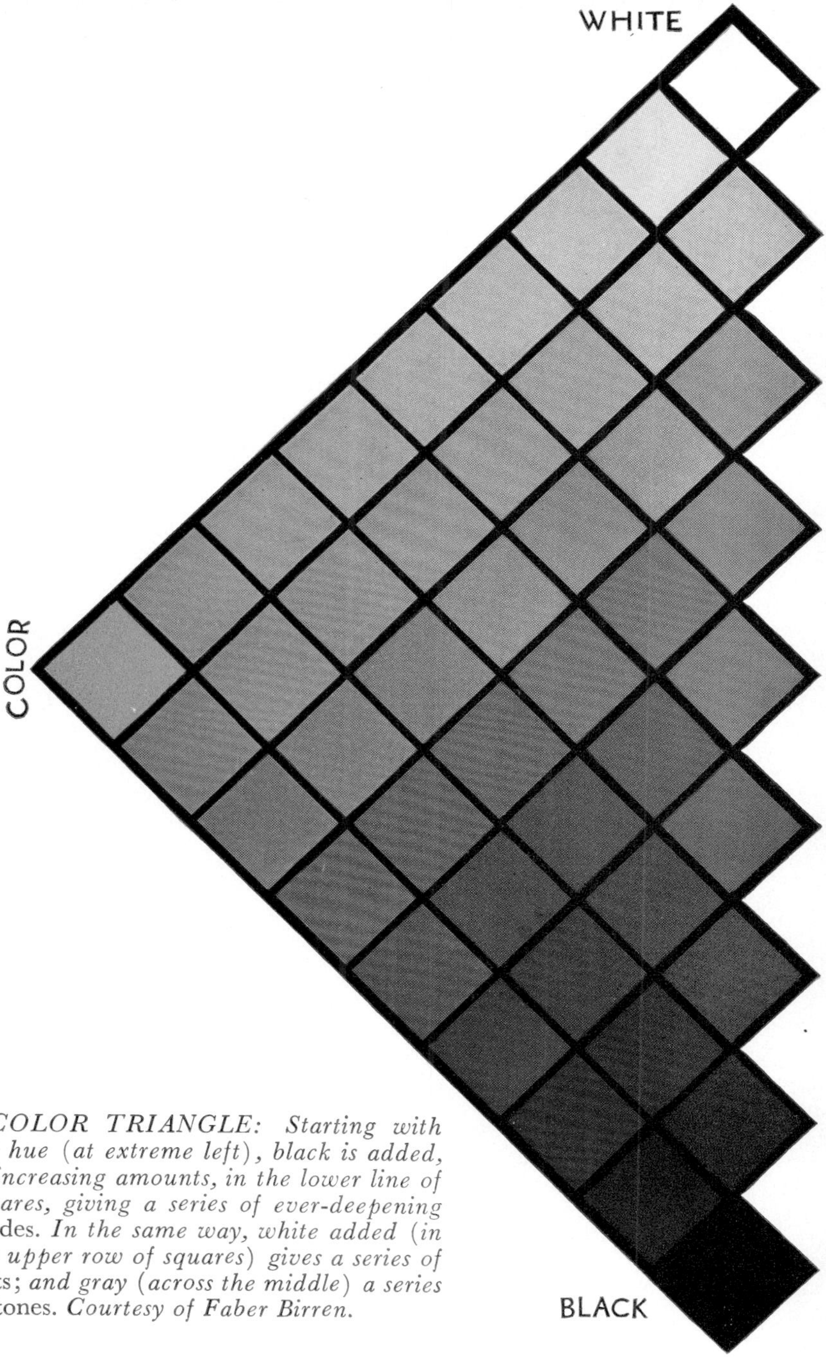

WHITE

COLOR

COLOR TRIANGLE: Starting with the hue (at extreme left), black is added, in increasing amounts, in the lower line of squares, giving a series of ever-deepening shades. In the same way, white added (in the upper row of squares) gives a series of tints; and gray (across the middle) a series of tones. Courtesy of Faber Birren.

BLACK

How to Use Color

If the above, on a first reading, seems rather complicated,

> *If the words seem queer*
> *And funny to your ear*
> *A little bit jumbled and jivey . . .*

don't be discouraged. Our purpose in dipping even thus gingerly into the color pot has been twofold: first, because flower-show schedules frequently call for arrangements carrying out a particular type of color harmony; second, because, in discussing color, a little knowledge is *not* a dangerous thing.

Don't feel that you must make every arrangement with flowers in one hand and a color circle in the other. In the first place, the colors of your flowers and those on the color circle won't jibe. The best you can expect to get is an approximation —but even that will help. *You will find it easier to get harmonizing combinations of flowers than of "color-circle" colors.* The reason for this is that few flowers come in strong, clear hues; and flower colors (tones, tints, and shades of the spectrum hues) are less likely to "fight."

A famous designer of floral bouquets maintained that flowers of any and all colors could be made to harmonize if sufficient foliage were used with them. That is more or less true, but often, for the sake of design, one does not wish to use much foliage. Gray-green foliage (such as that of the Mullein) will do wonders in making more harmonious those colors that do not quite click. Gray containers or gray backgrounds accomplish the same result. Neutral or "grayed" tones of any hue help in a similar way.

In placing flower arrangements in the home, lighting has a most important effect on color. The more direct and brilliant the light, the more intense—nearer to pure hues—will appear the colors, and the more dramatic the effect will be; *but,* by the same token, the more pronounced will be any lack of harmony in the colors used. So if you're not sure of your color combinations, experiment with more subdued lighting.

COLOR HARMONIES: *Study these in connection with the color circle. The examples reproduced here: above, monochromatic and analogous; below, complementary and triad.*

Arrangements by Mrs. Esther Wheeler, Mrs. Charles G. Scholz, Mrs. Gilbert nney, and Mrs. William A. Schuff

47

Constructing the Arrangement

There is much more to be said about the distribution and placement of color in the design, but we will leave that discussion for the latter part of this chapter. However, you needn't wait until you have mastered the subject to begin to play with color.

Get together such flowers and foliage as you can, and then try to plan an arrangement according to a *definite color scheme*. Examples of monochrome, analogous, complementary, and triad color harmonies in flowers are shown on pages 47, 53, and 123.

Illustrated on pages 106 and 108 are the progressive steps in putting an arrangement together.

First, the main line of the arrangement—which in this instance is also the dominant color (blue)—is put in place, held firm by a pinpoint holder in the bottom of the container.

Next, the focal point, or center of interest, is added. This includes, in this instance, the complementary color (orange) in the form of a large Tulip.

Finally, the filling in is done, with foliage and smaller flower sprays. Note how this not only completes and pulls together the design but also blends the color scheme and makes it more harmonious.

Don't be discouraged if your first attempts at getting pleasing color combinations fail to turn out as successfully as you hoped. In this phase of flower arranging, as in working out the design, practice must precede perfection, or any near approach to perfection. But the practice can be a lot of fun!

Bringing Color into the Arrangement

Up to this point we have attempted to present the theory of color in relation to its physical aspects, and establish in the reader's mind a simple but definite set of color terms instead of the more or less hazy terminology frequently employed—such words as "chroma," "notan," "value," "intensity," "pitch," "luminosity," and so on.

But just to pin this matter down definitely, and save the reader the trouble of referring to preceding pages, let us recapitulate here the color terms we have used, with their meanings, before we proceed to a further discussion of how to employ color most effectively in your arrangements.

COLOR. As used in a general sense, the subject of the spectrum hues, or their pigment counterparts; their variations, combinations, and uses.

COLOR. As used in a *specific* sense, any particular hue, around the color circle, such as blue, yellow, or red-orange (less accurately, to designate tones, shades, or tints of such hues).

SPECTRUM. The band of colors obtained by passing a ray of sunlight through a prism; these are "pure" colors.

FUNDAMENTAL COLORS. Those found in the spectrum. There are, according to different authorities, six or seven—red, orange, yellow, green, blue (indigo or purple), and violet.

PIGMENTS. Coloring matters, approximating the spectrum colors, used in making paints, inks, dyes, et cetera. (Nature supplies the pigments which give flowers their colors.)

PRIMARY COLORS. In pigments, the basic colors (red, yellow, and blue—or more, according to the system used) that are combined to give other colors; as blue and yellow, to produce green; red and yellow, to produce orange.

SECONDARY (INTERMEDIARY) COLORS. Those between the fundamental or primary colors on the color circle—such as yellow-orange or orange-yellow (see page 41).

HUE. A color of full strength on the color circle; i.e., approximating the same color in the spectrum.

SHADE. A hue made darker, as by the addition of black.

TINT. A hue made lighter, as by the addition of white.

TONE. A hue made duller, as by the addition of gray.

COLOR (CHROMATIC) SCALE. Any series of hues or of colors (such as tints or shades) arranged in gradual progression. The spectrum, a color circle, or any sequence in a color triangle, provides a color scale.

COMPLEMENTARY COLORS. Opposites on the color circle, which combine into white or neutral gray.

ANALOGOUS HARMONY. Colors adjacent on the color circle.

MONOCHROMATIC HARMONY. Shades, tints, and/or tones of the same *hue*.

The Psychological Side

These definitions (which have been presented at some risk of repetition, but in the interest of a clearer understanding of the subject) deal with the *physical* aspects of color.

But there is another side to color—the psychological. This is important to the arranger because it has a direct bearing on the *effect* which the arrangement will produce—the emotion it will evoke on the part of the observer.

Before you decide that this discussion is likely to soar off into the aesthetic substratosphere on a flight that is of no practical interest to you, just stop and look at the arrangement of red Gladiolus on page 297; and then refer to the monochromatic arrangement at the top of page 83.

Your reactions to these two arrangements may be subconscious, but you can scarcely fail to realize that the red Gladiolus produce a sense of cheerfulness, of motion and activity, that make them well adapted to the holiday season for which they have been selected. The most color-insensitive arranger in the world, on the contrary, would hardly choose the dull-toned dried foliage and twigs of the monochrome (beautiful in design though it is) for a Christmastime arrangement.

So discussion of the psychological values of colors is not just empty theoretical jargon. These values do have a practical, everyday application in the art of the flower arranger, even in so simple a matter as making bouquets for the home.

Reactions to Color

The use of color in decorating rooms, from the point of view of their psychological effect on those who live in them, has been given much attention during the last decade. It is generally recognized that some colors are stimulating, exhilarating; others actually depressing. We need not explore this interesting field far, but we can take a leaf or two from its book for practical application in the making of arrangements.

In general it may be said that the nearer we can get to pure hues (colors at their fullest intensity) the more attention-compelling and stimulating they are. Zinnias, for instance, come in intense colors, and a bowl of them on a sunny window sill will well demonstrate this point.

TINTS of the pure hues have a cheerful, uplifting effect; pink Roses combined with light blue Delphiniums would illustrate this. *Shades* have the opposite effect: in direct proportion as they approach black they tend to become depressing, especially if they are not counterbalanced by contrasting lighter colors. *Tones*—which, you will recall, are the result of "graying down" pure hues—are quieting, soothing in their effect. Many of the monochromatic arrangements made with dried material would fall into this category.

A comparable difference is to be found in respect to the several *hues* themselves, regardless of their intensity. Yellow, which we instinctively associate with sunshine, is a "cheerful" color; red suggests warmth; green, coolness; blue, tranquillity; violet, a touch of the spiritual, for want of a better word.

Now this digression into the psychological effects of colors is not intended to imply that when you think of making a flower arrangement you will sit down and decide, first of all, just what mood you want to throw the observer into as a result of his viewing it—and then go out and cut your flowers, or buy them, accordingly. It is, nevertheless, *usable* information that you will find it well to have stored in the back of your mind; it is one of several factors that will contribute to your ability to make better and more interesting flower arrangements. If you want a particularly cheerful bouquet—as one for a sickroom, for instance—you will not use blooms in somber shades; if you desire a cool effect in a shaded summer room, you won't go out and cut an armful of Paul's Scarlet Roses, or blazing red Gladiolus with which to accomplish your purpose.

Color in the Design

With this rather meager discussion of the psychological effects of color, let us now turn to the more practical matter of how to handle color in constructing an arrangement.

The first thing to keep in mind is that different colors have, or appear to have, different *weight* values. This is, of course, a mental illusion: a white Petunia and a dark purple one of the same size actually weigh the same, but the dark one *looks* heavier. This will become evident if you glance at John Brimer's sketches on page 55. Or, still better, take some flowers of light, medium, and dark hues, and do a little experimenting on your own.

Distribution of Color

When we talk of using color in the design of the arrange-ment, we are adding something to previous discussions of design. An arrangement in which colors are employed (as in most arrangements they are) is in reality a combination of two distinct designs—one of *forms,* the other of *colors.* We have, in effect, a design within a design. It is important, in discussing them, to keep these two types of design separated, although in the arrangement itself they are blended together. The sketches on page 54 illustrate what is meant by "a design within a design." In the first, light, medium, and dark hues have been used, hit or miss, in the arrangement. The result is a spotty, disorganized effect. In the second, the design of *forms* remains exactly the same, but the *colors* have been distributed with some thought as to the design which they themselves form.

The same principles which guided us in making a good design of *forms* apply to making a good design of colors. These

rrangement by Mrs. Esther Wheeler and Mrs. Charles G. Scholz

GARDEN BLOOMS IN ANALOGOUS HARMONY: For an
*analogous harmony, colors adjacent to each other on the color circle
are selected—such, for instance, as yellow, yellow-red, and yellow-
green, or (as in the arrangement above) violet, blue, and purple.
Here again one color (usually the "center" one) is used as the
dominant or key color and the others kept subservient to it. In
handling the distribution of the color, design, scale, balance, accent,
and the other general principles must be kept in mind.*

*The distribution of color within the composition should follow a defini[ ]
thought-out plan, thus forming a "design within a design." At left, abov[ ]
the different colors have been used in a hit-or-miss pattern, producing [ ]
spotty effect. As rearranged (right), they form a well-ordered pattern.*

are, as you will recall, scale, balance, harmony, focus, rhythm, accent, repetition, and unity. The only difference is that some of them are of relatively more importance as they apply to forms, others as they apply to colors.

SCALE. Proper scale, for instance, will be determined by the comparative sizes of the materials used, regardless of their colors. It is a most important factor in the *form* design, comparatively unimportant so far as color is concerned.

BALANCE, however, must be studied carefully in connection with colors as well as with forms. An arrangement that is satisfactory in its form design may be thrown decidedly out of balance by a careless distribution of colors. This is where it is important to keep in mind the apparent "weight" of different hues, discussed above. As a general rule it is desirable to keep the heavier (darker) colors fairly low down in the arrangement, or toward the center if it is a horizontal arrangement.

In attempting to secure good balance, in the distribution of colors, bear in mind that dark colors appear to weigh more than light ones. In the two arrangements above the form designs are identical, but improved feeling of balance is secured by placing the darker colors lower down (at right).

HARMONY. It is here that color plays a leading role. In flower shows, many an arrangement that is none too good in design is, as a result of good color harmony, pulled through to win a coveted prize. Color harmony is stressed in many classes in flower-show schedules, and exhibitors soon learn to realize its importance.

REPETITION. The artist who becomes skillful in the use of color will find frequent occasions when the principle of repetition can be employed to advantage. The importance of using repetition in connection with form and texture has already been emphasized. As it applies to color it is no less effective. Anyone who has attended flower shows and made even cursory examination of the prize-winning arrangements cannot have failed to notice how frequently this simple device, where used artistically, has been a factor in the decision of the judges.

In the photograph on page 29, the touches of creamy white in the foliage of the Variegated Ivy constitute a nice application of the principle of repetition. Repetition is *not* used artistically when it is carried to such extremes that it becomes as obvious as a bandaged thumb at a bridge party. We recall one instance in which a series of wooden disks, used to form a base for the container, had been painted in colors to match the flowers used in the container. This arrangement did not capture a blue ribbon!

UNITY. The foregoing discussion has been concerned primarily with the distribution of color within the arrangement itself. Unity, as we have said before, involves "the fitting-together-ness of *all* the component parts of a composition." To achieve unity in your flower compositions, therefore, it is not sufficient that the color scheme of the flowers alone be properly worked out. Containers, bases, and backgrounds should all be selected with just as great care, to make sure that they contribute their share to the creation of a harmonious whole. A study of the arrangements illustrated on pages 74 and 75 will show how, in each of them, the principle of over-all unity has been successfully carried out.

RHYTHM, too, must be carefully considered in working out the color design in an arrangement. The several colors used should form a definite pattern, and should flow into each other without leaving any effect of having been broken up or spotted in their application. Strong contrasts there will be, of course, especially in complementary harmonies. But that is something quite different from the hit-or-miss distribution of color throughout the arrangement.

Often the color design can be made to follow, more or less, the main lines (form-design) of the arrangement. This gives added emphasis to the lines, or rhythm, of the whole composition. Examples of this are shown in the photographs on pages 35, 157 and 207. These well demonstrate the added emphasis gained when form design and color design go hand in hand.

ACCENT. This brings us to the point of accent in the composition. As a general rule *one hue should be dominant—*

should set the key for the composition. Use enough of it so that there can be no question as to which is the "boss" color. If the color masses fight for the observer's attention, something is wrong; one color should be added to, or given a more prominent position (such as the focal point in the arrangement). It can be supplemented by other hues—either complementary or analogous—but these should all play subordinate parts. Or it may be supplemented by shades, tints, or tones of the same hue, producing a monochromatic color harmony.

Employing color as suggested above may be termed accent by mass effect. Equally important is accent by *contrast*. By means of this device, a very small part of the total color area of an arrangement may be thrown into such bold relief that it is the first thing to catch the eye. If, in addition to contrasting color, there is also contrasting form, the effect is heightened. A single flower may be made to dominate a whole bouquet. But the use of sharp contrast can readily be overdone. It should be employed only when well thought out, and when the contrasting color really fits into the color scheme of the chief area.

Focus. As a rule the focal point in the color design should coincide with the focal point in the form design. Otherwise there may result, on the part of the observer, a division of interest that will greatly detract from the over-all effectiveness of the arrangement. Frequently a complementary color may be employed at the focal point, but here again care must be exercised, for if the contrast is too sharply drawn it becomes a self-evident striving for effect, and thus defeats its own purpose.

Arrangement by Mrs. John Potter

Accessories that really add much to a composition are hard to find. Figurine used here is a perfect foil for the homey flowers (Geraniums, Primulas, Rose hips, and Maple branches) and the old
wooden bucket.

CHAPTER V

Containers, Accessories, and Backgrounds

Here is a basketful of flowers cut from your own garden, or a box from the florist. What are you going to put them in? What, if anything, will you use with them to supplement the arrangement? And where will you place it when it is done?

The answers to these three questions will have much to do with the over-all decorative effect you finally achieve. No matter how interesting your plant material—including foliage as well as flowers—nor how skillfully you can combine colors, you will fall far short of what you might do unless you acquire proficiency in selecting and using containers, accessories, and backgrounds. This applies to floral decorations for your own home no less than to arrangements for flower shows.

Choosing a Container

A "container" is flower arrangers' lingo for a vase (pronounced "vahze" if it cost more than twenty bucks), a jug, a bowl, a dish, a teapot, or what-have-you, in which flowers and foliage are placed. Again and again at flower shows we have seen the coveted blue ribbon go to an arrangement where the container—or, more accurately, the *suitability* of the container, in relation to the plant material used and its design—was the deciding factor in determining the award.

Each of the arrangements shown here is an integral part of the larger composition it forms with its immediate surroundings. In imagination change them about and note the results.

You may not be interested in making arrangements for a flower show—though the chances are that sometime you will want to try it—but the selection of the right container is no less important when you are making arrangements for your own home. *The container is just as vital a part of the picture you wish to create as are the flowers and foliage.*

Selecting the Right One

The beginner at flower arranging is not likely to have a large number of containers from which to choose. Part of the fun of making arrangements is to be found in gradually acquiring a number of different types and forms—a matter discussed at greater length later on. But even if you have available no more than three or four containers, *one* of them, for any projected arrangement, will be better than any of the others.

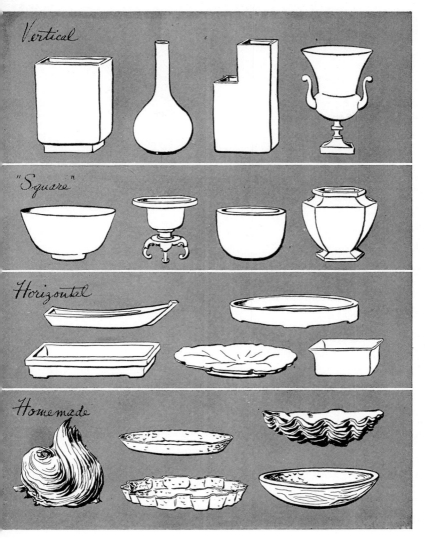

Vertical

"Square"

Horizontal

Homemade

JUST HOLDING WATER ISN'T ENOUGH. *Almost any vase, bowl,*
ug, or dish that will hold water will answer as a "container" for a flower
rrangement. The only trick is to select one which, with the flowers you're
rranging, will serve to help the success of the composition as a whole.
tart a collection of them. It's an intriguing hobby!

61

MASS. The mass arrangement, and its now more generally used modi fied form combining line and mass, require a suitably substantial con tainer of Occidental rather than Oriental design. It should be sufficientl; tall—about two-fifths of total height is usually the right proportion.

How can you tell which one is best? In a sense the answer is summed up in the one word *harmony*. But it is not quite so simple as that, for harmony in the relationship between the container and the plant material to be placed in it *and the arrangement of that material* is determined by several factors. Among these are scale, design, color, texture—and *spirit*. The latter is very difficult to define but nonetheless important.

SCALE. All that has been said concerning scale in preceding discussions of the subject applies to the size relationship between the container and the arrangement of plant material in it. A container too large for the over-all mass of the flowers and foliage tends to minimize the effectiveness of the arrangement and to center the attention of the beholder on the container. If it is much too large, the plant material will look ridiculously lost and out of place. If, on the other hand, the container is too small, the arrangement will appear unbalanced

PERIOD. The "period" arrangement—it may be Victorian, French, Colonial, or some other—calls for a corresponding period container. Even in the home, where one may ignore flower-show rules, a container of modern design, such as the one shown at the left, would be inappropriate.

and insecure; thus again, but for a different reason, the container rather than the flowers becomes the center of interest.

DESIGN. The next step in selecting a container that will be in harmony with your arrangement is to pick one whose general shape, or contour, will "look right" both with the general design of the plant material placed in it and, to a reasonable degree, with the form of the individual flowers. An arrangement with a circular design, for instance, would be much better set off in a container of rounded design than in one of rectangular shape. Often, too, the handles of containers can be made to contribute to the curved main line of an arrangement.

Large, boldly formed individual flowers call for a container of strong, simple design. Such flowers in a delicately wrought or elaborately decorated container would look out of place even though the latter might be correct in scale and harmonious in color.

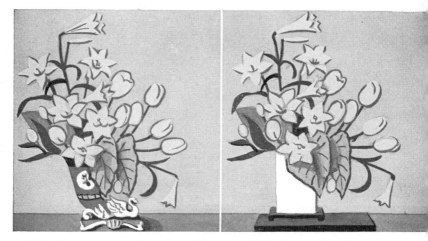

FORM and size of flowers and leaves will be factors in selection of container. Strong, dramatic flower shapes lose much when placed in a fussy, intricate vase (left), but gain when held in one of simple design (right). Container colors also should be plain and, in most cases, unobtrusive.

COLOR. The maintenance of harmony in the color scheme depends upon the container used no less than upon the plant material. No expert arranger, in planning a flower composition, ever thinks of the one without considering the other. As is the case with the flowers themselves, the color harmony may be worked out along the line of either analogous or complementary colors, but it should never be left to chance.

Very light or very dark containers, and those of neutral or pastel shades, in general will harmonize well enough with most flower combinations. But for the most striking effects, especially in competitive classes at shows, you cannot be too careful in making sure that the color harmony between the container and its contents is *just right*.

TEXTURE. What has been said in regard to color applies equally well in regard to texture; although here, if one has but a few containers, there may be less choice in the matter. It is

TEXTURE, too, is important. In left, above, there is a discordant note when smooth, broad-surfaced blossoms and foliage are combined with the ornate indented fruit dish. Harmonizing texture of container at the right corrects this fault and gives the arrangement much more distinction.

the harmony in *texture* (no less than in colors) that makes such rather coarse and bold flowers as Zinnias or Marigolds "go" with Mexican pottery the way maple syrup goes with pancakes; or such smooth and sophisticated blooms as Hybrid Tea Roses or Camellias seem properly set off by silver or glass.

Spirit. As we warned at the outset, that quality in the relationship between container and the arrangement of flowers within it which may be called "spirit" (for want of a better word) is difficult to define. It might be described as "atmosphere," or "unity." Where it exists, the observer will be moved by a feeling that in some subtle way container and material *blend* to create a single emotional response—to express a definite mood or thought. It is not often that this complete unity is achieved, but occasionally one comes across an arrangement that immediately evokes the feeling "here is perfection"

—and the wish that it might be preserved for many persons to enjoy for a long time to come instead of being doomed to almost immediate dissolution.

Fashions in Containers

Except for special purposes such as vases for "period" arrangements (of which more later), vases and dishes of neutral colors and simple forms are most useful. These set off the flowers without attracting too much attention to themselves and can be used over and over again with different flowers, yet never become tiresome. They are like "basic" dresses in contrast to striking individual costumes.

Containers of Oriental inspiration, even those made in the United States, are most apt to fill these requirements. The "pillow" container, for instance, shaped rather like a large brick set on end, is one of the best. Select it in antique white pottery, a pastel glaze, or heavy glass, and you have something which seldom fails you. The shallow oblong dishes of gray-green or old white pottery are also most useful. These usually have elementary legs or bases and hold enough water to keep flowers happy.

American potters do some nice things in shallow oval dishes without bases but with straight sides. Tall, straight-sided round jars or vases in bamboo, pottery, or glass have a wider usefulness than flaring jars, or vases pinched into a small opening. Gracefully blown bottles, with or without handles, show off single blooms or slender compositions better than the bud-vase type of thing. For Roses and exotics like Gardenias and Camellias you will want glass, china, or silver bowls, or deep open dishes, and low dishes of bubble or clear glass or of fine glaze.

PERIOD CONTAINERS are the vases belonging to a set period or style of arrangement. Unless you are going in for exhibition arrangements, these containers can wait until you want to increase your collection. Most of us have some old pieces of glass, china, or pottery which represent some of these periods, and it is fun to use them for flowers either at home or in shows.

Here again is a homemade container that makes the perfect foil for the plant material and accessories used with it. Charm, originality, and perfect unity.

There are, for instance, the ornate epergne used for Victorian flower groupings, the alabaster urns of classic design appropriate for French compositions, and the gold-encrusted porcelain vases of the Empire and the Regency. Quite different from these, but still "period" containers, are the simple stone jars, pewter jugs, and pressed-glass dishes of our American tradition.

If you are fortunate enough to own some genuine old vases or pitchers, spend a little time studying the sort of bouquets appropriate to these containers and use them when you can, in your own home or in competitive classes in flower shows.

It is surprising how many dishes, jugs, and household utensils can be successfully used to hold flowers if you are ingenious. The person who first thought of arranging flowers in a Cranberry picker proved that. Candle molds are often used for dried material, and at a recent show we saw half-a-dozen antique lamp bases used most effectively for Rose arrangements.

MODERN UTENSILS are just as interesting as antique ones. For a cocktail party why not arrange flowers in a cocktail shaker if the shape and color are appropriate? And for that matter a teapot or cream pitcher container appeals to us for a tea party even though many authorities contend these are not, strictly speaking, flower containers at all. Pickle jars and ginger jars have long been popular for coarse garden flowers like Zinnias and Marigolds. Chianti and other wine bottles seem to fit an arrangement for a man's room. Or place his bouquet in his golf cup if he has won one of the right shape and depth. In short, make use of whatever appeals to you, whether it is an open vegetable dish, a copper oilcan, or a milk jug.

When you reach the point where you really want to make a collection of containers, endless fun awaits your journeyings. The most unlikely secondhand shops may yield a treasure, while auctions are to be haunted and handmade potteries studied and compared. A trip to the woods may produce a twisted old root more beautiful than carving made by human hands, while the sea or lakeside yields silvery white driftwood or shells.

HOMEMADE CONTAINERS are worth while, too, if you are a craftsman. There was a famous container made of one large

Arrangement by Mrs. A. W. Jennings

No conventional container could give just the right
atmosphere to the idea the artist wished to express here.
This made-up container and the foliage selected provide
perfectly the desired prehistoric atmosphere.

polished bone which helped its owner win many prizes in the New York area, and we know of another such bone most gracefully carved with a frieze of draped female figures. Hand-hammered copper suits many flowers to a T, the coloring and texture being especially good with Begonia leaves, Chrysanthemums, and such. Wooden vases are not too hard to make but must be lined with a metal waterholder. And if a kiln is available, you may want to make some pottery vases yourself, either under class instruction or by studying methods in a book.

These are only a very few of the possibilities open when starting or rounding out your own collection. In addition, those arrangers who spend much of their lives exhibiting in shows are most skillful and ingenious at refinishing containers to suit a special need. Tempera colors or other cold-water paint can be used and washed off afterward. Often these temporary color effects are shaded from a pale to a deep shade, or are blended of several soft colors—rather like permanent pottery glazes except that the surface finish is dull instead of shiny.

Containers are really fun. Keep them on a special shelf where you can gloat over them. Before long they will demand a whole closet to themselves perhaps. Few of your household goods are likely to give as rich a return in beauty and usefulness.

Bases. A "base," as the word implies, is an object placed beneath a vase, a bowl, or any other container. Many containers, especially Oriental ones, are supplied with bases; these are often integral parts of the design. In selecting bases that do not "belong," one should consider carefully whether anything is gained in the artistic effect. Frequently a base will lend stability to an arrangement that seems top-heavy or otherwise out of balance (see page 177).

A base is not an accessory. It should be considered as a supplementary *part of the container*. That is its function both physically and as an element in the design. A well-chosen base may improve the composition. Where an accessory is used, a suitable base may help "tie the composition together," (see

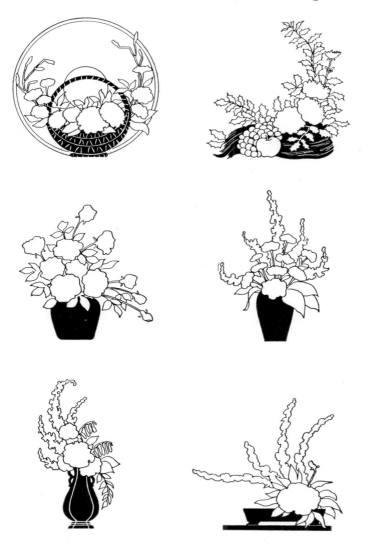

*The design followed in arranging the material should
harmonize with the design of the container.*

page 170); or it may add a conspicuous note of color harmony or contrast, or of repetition. But be certain your base *is* going to improve the composition before you decide to use one.

Accessories

In the preceding discussions of the principles and techniques of making flower arrangements there have been occasional references to accessories and backgrounds. Now it's time to take a closer look at these, for they are of vital importance in the final results the flower arranger achieves. Well used, an accessory may be a decided addition to the composition; or a well-selected background may add materially to its effect. Ill used, either one may detract from the desired effect, or even kill it.

Let's tackle the accessories first.

An accessory, in flower-arrangement jargon, is an object included in the composition but detached from, and supplementary to, the arrangement of plant material held within the container. It may be a book, a pair of gloves, a stray flower —or even a few fallen petals. Very often, if some such thing as a sugarbowl or a teapot is utilized as a container, the lid is employed as an accessory. Fruits of various kinds are frequently used as accessories because of the clear-cut form accents and the striking textures and colors they provide.

In some instances it is hardly possible to say just where the dividing line is between the arrangement proper and the accessory. Often an arrangement of fruits may "spill over" in such a way that one would have difficulty in determining whether any of them are or are not accessories. But this is an academic question which need not too greatly concern the beginner.

In painting, the employment of the accessory is of course an old device. But the artist, or would-be artist, who is working with plant material should bear in mind that he is at a great disadvantage—as compared with the artist who uses brush or pencil—when it comes to employing accessories. The painter can make his accessory exactly what he wants it to be in size, form, color, texture, and *emphasis*. The flower arranger is much more limited. It is very difficult to find a physical object that will in *all* respects just fit into the composition; and if in any one respect it is too far "out" it may prove a detriment rather than an addition to the composition.

Selecting the Accessory

On this and on the following pages there are examples of good and bad use of accessories. If you study them carefully, you should get a pretty good idea of what to *avoid* in selecting an accessory and to that extent at least set your feet on the right path. To pick just the right accessory is a more difficult task, because an object that would be a very desirable accessory with one arrangement is more than likely to be all wrong with another. But here are some of the considerations to be kept in mind.

First of all, never use an accessory just for the sake of using it. Unless it really contributes to the composition, *leave it out.* Exhibitors at flower shows, having seen blue ribbons go to arrangements supplemented by accessories, often get the idea that their chances of success would be increased by employing them. This is not true. More often than not an inappropriate accessory cuts down rather than increases the probability of winning an award. In the home, the use of such an accessory makes the general effect of the arrangement artificial if not actually ridiculous.

Before you decide to add an accessory to your arrangement —or, more correctly, incorporate it in the composition, for it should never be just "added to"—see that it passes these three basic tests: first, that it contributes to the design; second, that

CONTAINERS AND ACCESSORIES: In each of the arrangements on the following two pages, notice how the general design, form, color, and texture of flowers and leaves harmonize with the containers. In the flower arrangements in which accessories have been employed, they have been well selected for scale, character, and color harmony.

Arrangements by Mrs. Campbelline M. Russell, Jr., Mrs. Phyllis G. Shields, Mrs. Edith Alexander, and Mrs. Howard E. Andrews

Arrangements by Mrs. Mabel B. Smithers, Mrs. Homer Strong, Mrs. Laurie D. Webster, and Mrs. Homer Strong

DESIGN: *Here the accessory, instead of improving the composition splits it in two; built-up base also is too large in proportion to arrangement The same arrangement (of dried material and fruits) shown at right, i better without the over-large accessory, and with the smaller base.*

it supplements the theme or spirit of the arrangement; and third, that it harmonizes.

DESIGN. This is the first test. When you are tempted to work an accessory into a floral composition, ask yourself if it really helps the design, and give an honest answer! In Whistler's famous portrait of his mother, the framed picture on the wall is an accessory. In Van Gogh's "Woman from Arles" the green book on the table is in the same category. It takes no art critic to realize that in either case the omission of the accessory would have left a less well-balanced and less-interesting composition.

If your original conception of an arrangement—the mind's-eye picture that you have as it will appear when completed—*includes* an accessory, then you may feel reasonably sure that the accessory will be desirable. If the use of an accessory is an afterthought, you may feel equally sure that in all probability you will be better off without it.

DESIGN: Here again the accessories used (left) injure the composition: inkwell is too large, out of character; informal base inappropriate with formal container; picture on wall throws arrangement out of balance. Smaller accessories (right) carry out line of the design and add interest.

THEME. Frequently in flower shows the schedule for arrangements will provide a "theme" or idea which the arranger is supposed to express in his composition. Such classes are often farfetched, but they do have the advantage of adding variety, interest, and the opportunity for originality.

Under such conditions an appropriate accessory may go far in getting across the thought or the atmosphere which the arranger wishes to express or create. The reproductions on pages 58 and 81 are good examples. The right sort of accessory will also often give a fillip of humor, or even a bit of comic relief— sometimes much needed. This "theme" business, however, can readily be overdone, even in a flower-show schedule.

HARMONY. Deciding that an accessory in any particular case may be desirable, and then finding an accessory that will fill the bill, are, however, two quite different matters. Your accessory still has the third test to pass—that of harmony.

UNITY: In this composition (left) the accessory used is not a happy selection as there is no connection in theme between the spring garden flowers and ship. The little fawn is in the spirit of the arrangement, and also adds a touch of humor. The solid background does not disturb design.

Here there are a number of considerations to keep in mind. We get right back to our old friends, scale, color, texture, unity. *Because of the extra prominence which its very position gives it, any accessory must be examined with a particularly critical eye on all these counts.*

SCALE, of course, is the most obvious; and yet it is surprising how often one finds, even in large flower shows, accessories used which are obviously much too large or too small in proportion to the arrangements which they accompany.

If any accessory is sufficiently important—that is, desirable on most counts, but still out of scale—it may be possible to increase the dimensions of the arrangement, or (if the accessory is too small) to give it more apparent height by placing it upon a base, or to combine a secondary accessory with it. However, if this is attempted, exercise care to avoid an over-obvious result.

SCALE: In arrangement at left, accessory is out of scale (much too tall), also too dominating. Painted base, too, is incongruous with natural wood container. At right the accessory fruits and foliage are in scale; the connecting bamboo base helps to make them an integral part of the design.

COLOR AND TEXTURE. Needless to say the color of the accessory is quite as important as the color in the arrangement itself. It need not necessarily be of the same color, or colors, but if it does not harmonize—either in analogous or complementary colors—it will introduce a fatally discordant note.

The use of an accessory often provides the opportunity to "pick up" a color or colors used in the arrangement, and through *repetition* (see pages 74 and 75) gain additional emphasis and interest. But here again one must be careful, at the risk of defeating the end sought, to avoid the too obvious. In a recent exhibition we noted an accessory which had been painted to match exactly the color of the container. The result was—*blah*.

The above remarks concerning color apply with equal force to *texture*. Usually it is easier to find just the colors you are seeking in an accessory than just the right texture. When you can get both, you have the making of a ten-strike.

79

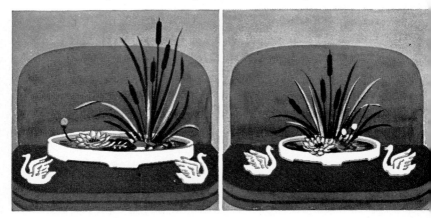

BACKGROUND: Where a table top, panel, or other definitely defined background is used take care to keep the arrangement in scale. The arrangement above (left) is too large for its "frame"; the smaller arrangement is a real improvement, but it would be better without any accessories.

The physical properties of your accessory, however, do not tell the whole story. It may be quite ideal in size, form, and coloring and still be something you would not, or should not, think of using. It has still to pass the final test of *unity*. Unity, as we have remarked before in these discussions, is a difficult thing to put your finger on—but it's important, nevertheless.

Backgrounds

Until you have actually tried placing an arrangement against different backgrounds, it will be difficult to realize how the background can alter the general effect of the composition. In flower shows, the backgrounds are usually provided, so there is not much that can be done about it except in classes where the exhibitor is permitted to provide a background.

In the home, however, it is a different matter. Here one of

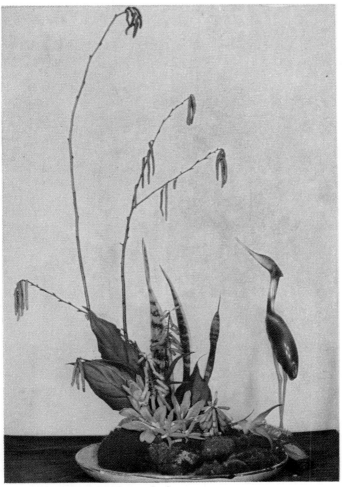

Arrangement by Mrs. Ernest L. Scott

Here's another excellent example of the perfectly selected accessory that becomes an integral part of the design, and by repetition of form and color adds a real punch.

BACKGROUND: *Here figured background makes it impossible to take in clearly the design of the arrangement, and accessories add to the confusion. Use of plain screen background and removal of accessories clear up the composition. The dark base gives design the stability it formerly lacked*

the most common mistakes is to place an arrangement in front of a window, with the light shining through it. Only a strong, bold silhouette arrangement will stand such treatment. The next most common mistake is placing an arrangement against a background—such as a figured wallpaper or screen—that absolutely confuses the design.

The *color* of the background, too, can go far in making or marring the arrangement. Try several different hangings behind one of your arrangements, and note how they change the effect (see page 83). A strong contrast, but one that is harmonious (i.e., of a complementary color), will give the most dramatic result, and is almost always desirable with arrangements that are viewed from a considerable distance. An analogous background, on the other hand, gives a subdued, quiet effect. A little experimenting will enable you to judge what type of background will be most desirable for the effect you wish to achieve.

BACKGROUNDS: *In the home no less than in the show backgrounds can add to or detract from your arrangements. These were done by Mrs. Lillian Norstad and Mrs. Ruby Y. Whitney.*

RIGHT   *WRONG*

RIGHT   *WRONG*

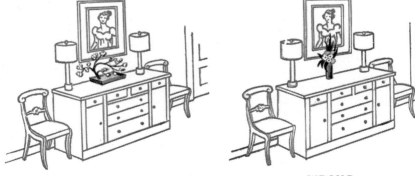

RIGHT   *WRONG*

Plan each arrangement to fit its assigned location. Design, scale, balance, harmony must all be considered. Which principle has been violated in each "wrong"?

CHAPTER VI

Selecting and Handling Materials

In this section on the selection of materials let us, first of all, emphasize the fact that the problem of the home arranger in regard to the plants with which she has to work is quite different from that of the artist who is securing flowers and foliage for show work. The latter is a specialized field. It sometimes involves sending to remote parts of the country—or the world—for rare, colorful flowers, unusual forms in seed pods, and unique foliage.

Some florists in our larger cities and in areas where women are particularly flower conscious cater to this trade. Experts in the exhibition field have a sixth sense about materials and are always on the lookout for what will serve their purpose. This is an excellent sense for any arranger to cultivate. If you instinctively possess it, by all means go in for competitive exhibition. You will probably make a success of it, whether you use "Wooden Roses," Spoon Cactus, Banana blossoms, or just some native wildling like Skunk-cabbage blooms in which you are perceptive enough to see possibilities. If you do not naturally think along these lines, try to do so and you will very possibly become so adept that you will find yourself a prize winner in flower shows.

By and large, most home arrangers depend upon the garden, the window garden, and the neighborhood florist, with a very occasional visit to the woods or fields. In the home you can make effective use of whatever you can grow or acquire without too much hardship. The simplest flowers can be combined to give pleasing—even striking—results. As your interest in arrangement grows, the garden plan each year will probably include more items especially adapted to this purpose. Your arrangements should improve in direct ratio to the time and thought you put on your plant material, if at the same time you study and practice the principles of good arrangement.

An amateur who specializes in one garden flower naturally learns to arrange this to the best advantage, and selects containers accordingly. Beautiful compositions can be and are made from such difficult subjects as Dahlias and Gladiolus. The woman with an old-fashioned garden and a Colonial house may go in for mass arrangements composed of Grandmother's flowers, and planned to suit Colonial interiors. The owner of a modern home plants Tritomas, Foxtail-lilies, and other flowers that are "modern" in spirit, and always has on hand a supply of such house plants as Callas, Monstera, and Fiddle-leaf Rubber Plant. An herbist may make a feature of Tuzzy-muzzys and other dainty, sweet-scented bouquets.

The first step toward making a pleasing arrangement is the selection of the materials—flowers, buds, foliage, branches, or sprays—that will form the design. Proficiency in this comes only with practice; every arrangement you make will prove to be another lesson in this direction.

There are two methods of procedure open to you: 1. You secure your flowers from the florist, the garden, or the wild, and let them suggest to your mind what kind of a flower design they are best suited to. You then pick out a container and go to work; 2. You have a container or containers of certain sizes, shapes, and colors, and positions in your living rooms where one of these can be used to advantage. You consult the surroundings, the spirit of the room, and the texture, shape, and color of the container you select, and then you secure the flowers which you think will create the best effect. In this case you will buy or cut flowers or other material not only of the right size and color but, if possible, of the right curves to carry out the design you have in mind.

The second method is the one used by those who wish to make really outstanding arrangements either for the home or for exhibition purposes. The first is apt to be used by those who go out into the garden and cut whatever is in bloom at the time. It must necessarily be employed also by anyone who receives a box of florists' flowers as a gift.

What to Select

Whether you are buying flowers or cutting them yourself, choose each individual bloom or branch carefully if you possibly can. If you are planning an asymmetrical arrangement, remember whether the long horizontal lines are to be on the right or on the left and choose sprays which "face" the right way. You will want long-stemmed buds or spike flowers for height. If you are working with a curving pattern, do not use branches of accessory material which branch out at a sharp angle. Select something like Broom or Wisteria which grows naturally in great, free curves.

Sometimes when buying florists' material you can get a lower price on flowers the stems of which are not straight. These will serve your purpose best. The reason that hothouse Roses are so hard to arrange is because every stem is as straight as a ramrod and every bud at an equal stage of development. The best thing to do with such flowers is to combine them with other material which will soften the general stiff effect and pull the composition together. The exhibitor may use Lilacs, Stocks, and Anemones. The home arranger can substitute forced sprays of flowering shrubs, Pussywillows or the soft foliage of Maidenhair Fern, or one of the smaller-leaved Scented Geraniums. *Pelargonium crispa variegata* is as colorful as a flower and has a delightful lemon scent as well, but it is sometimes hard to come by.

Select flowers and foliage to harmonize with the spirit, shape, and texture of the container in which they are to be placed, and the position they are to occupy. In color you will want either a similar color or a good contrast.

Quality

Another important point in the selection of cut flowers is their quality. This should be of the best, whether the blooms come from the florist or from the garden.

Though it pays to economize by choosing curving stems and informal flower spikes or heads when buying, it never pays to purchase blooms which are not strictly fresh, of good color, and with crisp foliage and stems of good stamina. With stale or low-grade material you have lost the fight before you start.

The same thing applies to garden flowers. Choose the best the beds and borders afford—unblemished blossoms, strong stems, and fine foliage—if you really want lovely effects and hope to have your arrangements hold up well.

In winter. During the cold weather, when flowers must come from the florist, you can make a small expenditure go a long way by supplementing a few bought blooms with:

1. Dried material, such as Bayberry branches or dried Wisteria vines with their graceful curves.

2. Evergreens from the garden like Rhododendron, conifers, or English Ivy.

3. The foliage of house plants—kept on hand for the purpose.

4. In late winter branches of forced flowering shrubs.

Care of Florists' Flowers

When a box of flowers arrives from the florist, do not be carried away by their beauty to the point where you arrange them at once, possibly in shallow containers.

First of all, look at the stem tips. If the severed ends are dark—not freshly cut—recut each stem on a slant with sharp pruning shears. Next fill roomy buckets with cool water and plunge the flowers deep. Let them rest in a cool, preferably dark room in deep water for several hours. At the end of that time arrange them.

Arrangement by Mrs. J. Lloyd Berrall

KEEP THEM FRESH! Even tapering spikes of flowers, such as Snapdragons, Stocks, Lilacs, and Delphinium, will stay put if they have been properly "hardened." Many a blue ribbon is lost because of drooping blossoms.

In the case of exotics, like Gardenias and Camellias, leave the cut blooms in the florist's box and keep in the refrigerator until ready for use.

How to Cut and Care for Garden Flowers

As all dirt gardeners and flower arrangers will tell you, there is more to cutting and keeping flowers for the house than just dressing up in a sheer cotton frock and a floppy hat and making a magazine cover of oneself in the Tulip or Peony bed.

Because we know that cut flowers do keep fresh for days in water, we are often inclined to treat them carelessly and to expect too much of them. The blossoms do mighty well to live at all after being severed from the plants, and the least we can do is to give them the very best breaks possible.

When to Cut. Very early in the morning, or, better still, after sundown at night, is the best time for cutting garden flowers. Hot sun is death to them, while a high wind or even a stiff breeze may break or bruise petals. If you have reason to think that a heavy storm is brewing with beating wind and rain, cut as many flowers as you can handle conveniently indoors. During really bad weather they will last better cut than in the garden. This is particularly true of hardy bulbs such as Daffodils and Tulips; of heavy-headed blooms like Peonies, and of hardy Chrysanthemums in late fall when storms or low temperatures may strike.

Unless the day is very cool and moist, it is wise to carry a bucket of water with you when cutting. It is less artistic than a flower basket, but placing the newly cut stems at once in deep water may prolong the life of the flowers for several days. Do not crowd many blooms into one bucket or you will find it impossible to remove them without tearing and bruising the petals. Give each flower headroom so that foliage, side stems, and petals do not become entangled with others. Several trips can be made with the bucket to the dark, cool cellar or potting shed where the flowers are placed in deep jars of water to "harden" for several hours or, better, overnight.

How to Cut. Use sharp stem cutters or pruning shears and snip each stem on an angle so that it will not adhere closely to the bottom of the container and thus prevent water from being absorbed. Hard-wooded shrubs or branches of half-hard wood should be split a few inches up from the base to facilitate water intake. In cutting for arrangements, see that at least half the flower stems are as long as may be without damaging or weakening the plants from which they come. You may need height when working out the design. Select flowers in bud or partly open if you want them to last some days indoors. (A few full-blown blossoms may be needed at once near the base of the composition and these will probably have to be replaced before the rest of the arrangement fades.)

Dr. Alex Laurie has this to say in *Making Your Cut Flowers Last Longer:*

The shortness of life of most cut flowers is proverbial, and rightly so, for after all the functions of a bloom cease as soon as pollination takes place and the development of a new generation starts. For many years all sorts of attempts were made to prolong this period in the life of the plant and make flowers cut off from the plant last longer by precautions and artificial measures.

These precautions are based on the fact that flower stems must take up water and thus remain turgid as long as possible. To make sure that water intake takes place, we must first learn just where this water enters. Studies have shown that water is taken up into the stem through the cut surface only. As a consequence it is important that this cut surface be as large as possible, and secondly that the conducting vessels do not become plugged. To attain the first end the *cuts made should be slanting* and not square across, using a sharp knife and not scissors which crush the stem in cutting and reduce the intake areas. In case of hard-stemmed flowers, such as Chrysanthemums or Stocks, the mere cutting is insufficient and actual splitting of the stem for an inch or more is necessary. The same treatment is used for branches of flowering or other shrubs, trees, evergreens, et cetera.

The second effort—that of preventing the clogging of the conducting vessels—is done by disinfecting the water to prevent the rotting bacteria from gaining a foothold, by cutting stems under water, by the removal of excess leaves from the base of the stem, by changing water daily. Let us discuss these individually.

Disinfectants to be effective must be strong enough to keep the water sterile. Unfortunately most of the ones recommended are worthless—such as aspirin, Listerine, vinegar, et cetera. Yet if we were to use those strong enough for the purpose, some damage is sure to be done to the stem, so it's not advisable to bother with them, although copper compounds have been found somewhat useful. This was the reason why some workers advocated the use of copper containers. Our findings show that this rarely helps.

The cutting of stems under water is based on the assumption that, if cut in the open, air bubbles are apt to form in the bases of conducting vessels and thus prevent water intake. Continuous tests have not shown this to be true and we think the method is worthless. Cutting the stems properly and immediately immersing in water is fully as satisfactory and much more convenient.

The removal of excess foliage and the change of water daily are actually helpful and should be practiced. There is no rotting of the submerged leaves and by using fresh water accumulations of tissue-decomposing bacteria are reduced.

Another important method of increasing the keeping quality is to reduce the transpiration (evaporation of water) from the foliage. Most flowers absorb a maximum amount of water while in a fresh condition. As soon as transpiration exceeds the amount of water entering the stem, wilting and death occur. The situation is relieved first by making sure that water intake is not impeded and secondly by elimination of heat and draughts, which accelerate the rate of water loss from the leaves. Thus, *keep the cut flowers cool, out of the sun, and away from draughts.*

Despite all these precautions little was done to actually prolong the life of cut flowers until the writer and his assistants found several years ago (1936) that the important thing was to prevent quick maturity. So instead of using disinfecting materials, chemicals were selected which would actually stop or retard some of the life processes (respiration). At present we are recommending two different formulas which work.

Formula 1. Make a stock solution of *hydrazine sulphate* by dissolving 1 ounce of it in 1 quart of water. In using take ¼ cup to 3 gallons of water and to each quart of water add 2 tablespoons of sugar. Roses, Carnations, Chrysanthemums, and many others respond to this well. Where used no daily changes of water are needed.

Formula 2 (developed because of difficulties in obtaining hydrazine sulphate during the war) serves as a satisfactory substitute. It consists of ¼ teaspoon of alum (potassium aluminum sulphate), ¼ teaspoon of Chlorox (sodium hypochlorite), ⅟₁₆ teaspoon ferric oxide, and 2 teaspoons of sugar—all to 1 quart of water.

If you don't care to bother with these preparations, two trademarked materials of similar composition are on the market, and both of them work very well—Bloomlife and Floralife.

To be more specific, upon arrival of flowers from a florist, or after being cut from the garden, (1) cut stems with a long, slanting cut; (2) immerse as deeply as possible in cold water; (3) remove to the coolest place you have (45–50° F. is an ideal storage place, with high humidity); (4) after this storage for an hour or more make your arrangement. (Incidentally, because of the intake of water through the base of the stem largely, flowers will keep just as well in a shallow bowl as in a deep vase, unless the atmosphere is extremely dry.)

If flowers arrive in a *wilted condition,* the *cutting of stems* and *plunging deeply in cold water* will revive them. Corsages, after being worn, may be sprinkled, placed in *airtight cellophane bags,* and kept in a refrigerator, and will be useful again for another occasion. Usually the *shorter the stem* the *longer the lasting quality.* Thus, after the first day, you may cut off several inches of the stem and continue to do so daily.

Some kinds require special treatments. Poinsettia, Heliotrope, and Euphorbia stems should be *singed* over a flame or dipped in *boiling* water for a minute before plunging in deep water. The same applies to Oriental Poppies. Although the same treatment has been suggested for Dahlias, better results are obtained by placement in *warm water* and allowing it to cool normally, or actually plunging them up to the flower base in *ice-cold water.*

In general, it should be remembered that temperature and humidity play an important part in prolonging the keeping qualities of flowers, so that no matter what precautions are taken, flowers will not keep long in hot, dry rooms.

And now, having digested the very latest scientific data on making flowers last, written by one of the country's leading authorities, we can go on to the next step in flower care.

Transporting

When entering in the arrangement classes of a flower show, it is important to transport your material with great care, since torn petals or marred stems count against the exhibitor. Pack the flowers carefully in a box, keeping the blossoms separated from each other with wax paper. Very delicate blossoms, such as Iris, must be moved in an upright position and not touching. Stuff the compartments of a deep, subdivided carton with wet newspaper or Sphagnum Moss and force each stem into these separately so that all are held rigid.

How to Prepare Material for Arranging

As you arrange the "hardened" flowers, remove one at a time from its container of water, cut the stem to the desired length, remove any foliage which would be submerged (in order to prevent decay), and see that the newly cut stem goes back immediately into water. Blooms which lie about on the table while others are placed soon lose their freshness.

Stems which rest against the bottom or sides of a container should be recut each day. If they are set in a pinpoint holder, the sharp pins keep the pores open and recutting is not so necessary.

PRUNING, CUTTING, BENDING, AND SPLICING. After the material has been "hardened," you are ready to make your arrangement. If a pottery, metal, or other opaque container is used, remove all foliage from that part of the stems which will be under water. Water-soaked foliage rots quickly and the decay spreads to the stems and flowers.

In using sprays of shrubs or trees or many-branched flower stalks, it is usually necessary to prune away confusing cross branches and excess leaves. Especially in the main or skeleton lines of your arrangement (usually three dominant branches or sprays about which the rest is built), you will want clean, flowing curves not confused by twigs or leaves in the wrong place.

Most of the stems used will have to be recut to make them the exact height needed. Measure each carefully against the container and cut at an angle. Stems cut at an angle cannot cling to the bottom of the vase and so water is absorbed more freely.

Very often a branch, spray, or stem is not curved just as

we should like it. With patience this can be remedied. Very gentle stroking and bending with the fingers coax a soft stem into a new curve (see page 103). If any of the fibers are bruised or crushed, however, the stem will break over. Woody material like Willow and Broom can be immersed in water for some hours, then bent to the desired curve and tied there until "set."

When using a tall opaque container it is sometimes possible to splice a short stem below the water line. Select a stout twig or cut stem and fasten it firmly to the stem to be spliced, using florists' twine or wire or a Twistem (green paper-covered wire binder).

If you want to use Waterlilies in an arrangement, a drop of paraffin at the base of the petals will keep them from closing. When garden Lilies are to feature in a bouquet, remove the stamens as soon as the blooms are cut. Lily pollen stains the petals themselves when it falls, not to speak of your hands, dress, or tablecloth.

WATERING. After the first long hardening off in deep water in the dark, cut flowers take their place in the house, in vases or other containers. Those which hold plenty of water are preferable to prolong life and freshness. Flowers cannot thrive many days in a flat dish which holds only a fraction of an inch of water. Shallow dishes should be kept full of water at all times. With a bulb syringe, remove the stale water from all containers each day and give a fresh drink. Be sure that no stems have become displaced so that they are out of the water.

LOCATION OF ARRANGEMENTS. Do not arrange flowers or place finished compositions in a drafty or sunny place or near a radiator, stove, or steampipe. Give them cool positions in full light but no direct sunshine, and in hot weather remove them, if possible, during the fierce heat of the day to a table in a cool, dark room or cellar free from the debilitating effect of high temperature and close, exhausted air.

CHAPTER VII

Mechanics of Arranging

We have talked at some length about the theory of arranging flowers—the principles of good composition, the use of color, the selection of materials; and the preceding chapter gave suggestions on selecting flowers and foliage and so handling them as to keep them fresh as long as possible. Now we are ready to take up in detail the *mechanics* of the art—the tools and techniques which experienced arrangers employ to get just the results they seek to accomplish.

Even if you've never attempted really to arrange flowers, you've undoubtedly had the experience, when placing them in a vase or a bowl in the most informal manner, of having them prove extremely obstinate about staying put where you wanted them. If you have endeavored to carry out the exercises suggested up to this point you will have noticed the same thing. At flower shows you must have wondered how blooms and foliage in intricate designs were kept in place, and fresh. That is just where the mechanics of arranging come in.

Equipment

The essential equipment for the arrangement of flowers consists first of a collection of containers which will fill all possible requirements. A very few can fill the bill at first if they are of neutral colors and various shapes and sizes. Chapter V gives further details on this subject.

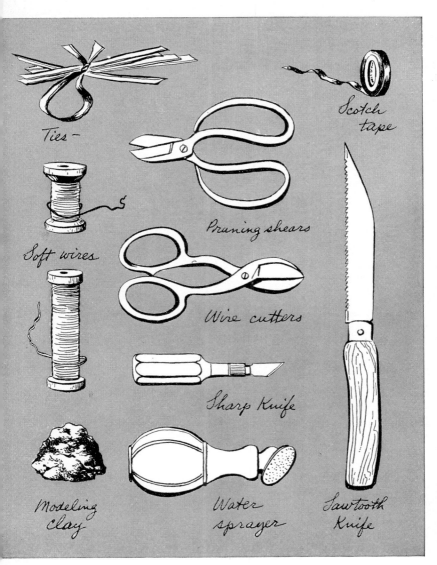

Ties —

Soft wires

Modeling Clay

Pruning shears

Wire cutters

Sharp Knife

Water sprayer

Scotch tape

Sawtooth Knife

Some gadgets and materials that are helpful in preparing and putting together cut blooms and foliage in making flower arrangements. You'll find it wise to keep them all assembled in one place.

Next you will need a good solid table or counter which is not marred by water standing on it. In good weather I arrange at an outdoor table in the shade to avoid the mess in the house.

Have plenty of roomy buckets to hold the plant material. If it is not crowded together the job is cut in half. Place tall sprays in one pail, buds in another, full-blown flowers in a third, and accessory foliage in a fourth. This saves time in the end.

On the table, conveniently arranged, place the equipment which, when not in use, is kept in an accessible cupboard or drawer.

Frances Coffin Gaskill, expert arranger, has this to say on the subject of equipment and the mechanics of flower arrangement:

First to be considered are the props to mechanics. Much time and irritation are saved if these are collected in *one* convenient place and not scattered about in cupboard, drawer, and box. I find it a good plan to give over one pantry drawer and the adjacent cupboard to the materials of my hobby.

In the drawer I store all my lead-base, needlepoint holders which, in a variety of shapes—squares, circles, oblongs, and crescents—make arranging pleasant. I have found such holders the most reliable and worth-while type, so I have collected them from Honolulu to New York.

In the same drawer, on a ready-to-move 14″ by 20″ tray, I keep all my arrangement tools. These include:

Small clippers	*Green pipe cleaners*
Scissors	*Small bottle of 3-in-1 oil*
Bunch of raffia	*Bottle of white shellac*
Modeling clay	*Package white cotton co-ets*
Chewing gum	*Small paint brush*
Twistems—4-in. and 8-in. sizes	*Jar of protective hand cream*
Wooden chopsticks	

Many of these gadgets come from the dime stores, but my well-sharpened clippers and scissors are the best that money can procure. A clean, neat cut made straight across saves flower stems and makes it easy to fasten them on the needlepoint holders. If stems are woody or thick, a crisscross vertical cut is also made so that the stem can be forced on the spikes without too much pressure.

The bunch of 7-inch raffia is secured by a rubber band, so that a strip may be pulled from either end without having a frustrating unraveling of the whole. This raffia is used for tying small bunches of thin-stemmed flowers together for firm placement. Tulip stems will not curl away from the spikes of the holder if they are tied first, and any stem such as Snapdragon, or even Gladiolus, that has a tendency to split when placed on the spikes acquires added tensile strength from a raffia tie. All tying is done at the base of the stem where raffia is wrapped around firmly several times, tied in a double knot, and both the ends cut off neatly.

If a needlepoint is not heavy enough for such plant material as a Magnolia branch, for example, I first cover the base of the holder with a thin layer of modeling clay before pressing it firmly to the bottom of the container. Container, holder, and clay must be

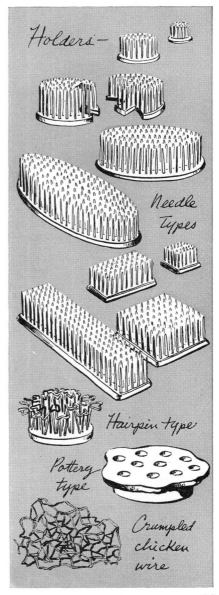

Holders —

Needle Types

Hairpin type

Pottery type

Crumpled chicken wire

absolutely dry, however, or they will slip and slide instead of adhering. If large, heavy needle holders are not available, small ones anchored in this way carry unexpectedly heavy weights. Sometimes, too, with heavy branches I make doubly sure by placing on the firmed needle holder several small inverted holders just to increase the ballast.

Chewing gum is an indispensable if inelegant prop. I learned about it from an exquisitely gowned lady, who, at one of the big shows, attracted my attention by her violent and incongruous chewing as she sat working upon an arrangement she was preparing for exhibition. Rhododendron leaves were involved and they were refusing to assume any but the most uncompromising right-angle curves. So the lady persuaded them by fastening her well-chewed wad as a weight just inside the tip of the determined-to-jut leaf which she intended should hang gracefully over the lip of the container.

The 4-inch Twistems (patent plant ties) are used as splints. They come to the rescue for a bent or partially broken stem which is too vital to be discarded. One may be laid in back and another in front of a Delphinium spire and fastened top and bottom with the finest wisp of raffia. When the splint is concealed by a leaf or flower, who would guess the accident that might have been a fatality?

Sometimes, too, by means of Twistems, a good material can be created from poor or mediocre stuff. This is helpful if a schedule calls for something your garden or your florist cannot supply at top quality.

The larger Twistems can also be fashioned into an emergency holder for an upright vase. If the neck is wide and the flowers flop to one side, I fit the vase top thus:

Cut two pieces of heavy flower stems (or chopsticks, if these are available) just a fraction longer than the diameter of the mouth of the vase. Cross these at right angles and wrap the crossing point firmly with Twistems. Then wedge this contrivance about an inch below the top of the vase. This creates four pie-shaped openings instead of one large unmanageable space.

When a tall vase is wanted, but stems are too short to display the flowers well, another workable device is to fill the vase part way up with sand, pebbles, tightly packed tissue, or newspaper, as a support for a needle holder into which the short stems may then be inserted.

Pipe cleaners, fastened to weak stems or to the midribs of weak leaves, are also dependable strengtheners. Their soft green color renders them invisible.

Chopsticks, like Twistems, do double duty, since they may be used to lengthen too short stems or be tied to Orchid tubes that hold short-stemmed flowers. These tubes are completely concealed by the mass arrangements in which they are used. Stability is insured by tying with raffia in two places instead of one.

The white cotton co-ets on my tray are on hand to apply the smallest quantity of oil to leaves that need cleaning and polishing. Galax, Ivy, Magnolia or Rhododendrons come out in new beauty under this simple treatment, while a coat of white shellac adds days to the life of fruits or vegetables. I also have shellacked the interior of several too porous containers through which moisture seeped to the detriment of the furniture.

Another discovery I have made is that when the first branches or stems are being inserted half the battle for balance and stability is won if the tip of the main placement is set directly over the base. With this accurately and firmly anchored, the subsequent "fill-in" work will not upset the arrangement. I have also discovered (the hard way, too, I must admit) that a wobbly start means inevitably a wobbly ending. It is most important that the holder be strong and firm enough to do what is expected of it.

Other methods of holding stems in position practiced by many arrangers are:

1. Place a piece of crunched two-inch chicken wire in a vase and fit the stems snugly into the holes.

2. Stuff the vase with cut Ferns inserted vertically.

3. A woody stem can be held in place by splitting its base and forcing into the crotch a crosspiece or wedge just long enough to fit neatly across the bottom of the vase.

4. In low open dishes, small rocks can be used to help steady a group of stems set in a holder. Pebbles or glass marbles are sometimes used though these are more to cover the holder, which should never be visible.

5. Strips of flexible plumber's lead in widths from one-fourth to one inch can be very useful for holding stems in place. Especially in a mass arrangement or where heavy material overlaps the rim of the vase, lead strips are indispensable. Wrap the strip about the stem or group of stems just below the rim. The lead must be completely hidden by foliage or flowers.

CHAPTER VIII

Constructing the Arrangement

With materials, flowers, and container assembled, and a fairly clear mental picture of what the arrangement is to be, we come to the final and exciting step of actually putting the arrangement together.

Here your first attempts are bound to be rather faltering, but with each arrangement you make you will find yourself gaining in confidence and sureness of touch. Little tricks with bending stems, removing just the right surplus leafage or side branches, or even so simple a thing as fastening the bases of stems *securely* into pinpoint holders, will become easy, and you'll wonder why you had so much trouble with them during your first attempts.

First of all, provide yourself with sufficient space on which to work—room enough to spread out your material, so that any flower or bit of foliage can be picked up readily without disturbing those that remain.

The actual putting together of the arrangement will progress by a series of trial-and-error operations. The first step is to establish the main lines of the arrangement—the backbone which will determine its dominant design no matter how much or how little is added to it afterward. But before the first (which is usually the tallest and most important) of these flowers or branches is put in its permanent place, hold it in approximately the position it is to occupy, and check it carefully for height and for "curve." The correct height and curve

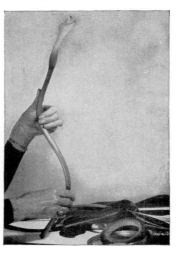

STEMS: Above, Calla, as cut; and bending stem by gentle, repeated pressure to obtain just the line wanted. Flowers and foliage are then "made up" in advance, to save time in assembling arrangement at show. At right, completed arrangement in place. Leaves under water hide stems; lighting simulates sunshine; glass brick base is harmonious.

Demonstration by Mrs. Anne Elizabeth Erhorn

will be determined primarily by the size and form of the container. Then cut it to the exact length wanted, and secure it in the holder.

It is vitally important that this first branch or flower be made absolutely firm. If at all "wobbly" it is practically certain to cause trouble later on. We have seen more than one arrangement at flower shows lose its chance of achieving an award because of the material shifting position; and even with a strictly made-for-the-home arrangement there is nothing more exasperating than to have the nascent work of art suddenly begin to go to pieces just as it nears completion. If the holder itself is not sufficiently heavy to keep the arrangement firm and steady, it should be secured to the bottom of the container with floral clay (see pages 99 and 100).

With the first main line established, the next step is to add the secondary or supplementary main lines. In the case of an oriental design (see page 149) these will be the "man" and "earth" lines; in a symmetrical pyramidal design (see page 150) the strongest of the supporting lines on either side of the upright; and in the case of a curved-"line" design (see page 146), the supplemental curves—in reverse, if a "lazy-S" or Hogarth curve is to be employed.

Here again each piece of material should be held in position for checking before its exact length is determined and the final cut made. This can be done much more easily and accurately if the material is viewed against a plain neutral background that will cause it to stand out in sharp silhouette. Also it should be viewed at approximately eye level; looking down on the arrangement, while putting it together, may throw it very much out of proportion.

Now is the time to do any bending of stems, or stiffening of leaves with wire and parafilm to make sure that each will assume *and hold* the exact position wanted, at the same time making certain that no artificial support is obvious from the angle at which the arrangement will be viewed. Any artificial bracing or stiffening—while permitted in flower-show work—should be regarded as a necessary evil, a sort of poetic license allowed the flower artist.

FOLIAGE: Large leaves can be made to stand upright, or assume desired curves, by using florists' wire, held in place by Scotch tape or parafilm, on the reverse side. (In photograph, white paper is used, as parafilm would not show.) Below: finished arrangement— wired foliage held erect instead of flopping; wings on figurine carefully painted to pick up color of the Anthuriums.

Demonstration by Mrs. Anne Elizabeth Erhorn

Flowers and foliage for main lines are cut or bent to the desired curves, and secured in a heavy holder placed in the container.

Shorter-stemmed flowers are used to complete the curve; and a center of interest is added by one large or several small blooms.

While many of the most stunning and artistically perfect arrangements at the big flower shows could not be achieved without the technique which employs such artificial mechanical devices, the less there need be of them the better. In making arrangements for home decoration there is seldom the temptation to use the extra time and care which such devices involve. In the home, moreover, the charm of naturalness and simplicity is likely to outweigh any increased perfection of design; therefore quite frequently more will be lost than gained in so striving for the latter that one must employ extreme means to attain it.

Focal Point. The arrangement now begins to take definite form and shape, and the next step, in most instances, will be to add the focal point or center of interest. Sometimes, however, this is left to the very last; it all depends on the type of material and the way the arrangement is going together. Where

Smaller flowers and foliage are used to fill in and to break horizontal line of container—but be careful you do not overdo this.

The completed arrangement, placed on a stand that is in scale (in size) and in harmony (in color and texture) with it.

a single large flower, or a group of smaller ones—or of fruits, for instance—provides a definite focal point, it is often the last thing added.

One of the most common errors in providing the focal point in an arrangement is to get it too large—out of scale. Another is to fail to have it in harmony—in color, form, or texture—with the rest of the arrangement. Both of these mistakes are frequently made by those who have had considerable experience no less than by beginners. Take particular care that the focal point is such that it will not defeat its own purpose. It should be the center of interest; it should *not* be so dominating that the rest of the arrangement becomes merely a background for it. (For good examples of well-selected and well-placed focal points see the arrangements on pages 29, 131, and bottom of 151.)

1. THE MATERIALS   2. MAIN LINE

CONSTRUCTING AN ARRANGEMENT: Shown above are the steps usually followed in putting an arrangement together. First comes the selection of materials and container; next, the blooms, sprays, or foliage that will determine the main line are placed; then the center of interest (focal point) is added; and finally the "filling in" is completed. The

FILLING IN. The arrangement now nears completion, but the few remaining details will go far toward making it or marring it. They might be considered under the heading "Subtraction and Addition."

Before adding the last few touches that will complete the job, look it over carefully and see what you can *take away*. One arranger who is a consistent winner of blue ribbons, asked to give the secret of her success, replied tersely, "Knowing what to leave out."

3. *FOCAL POINT*   4. *FILLED IN*

*olor scheme should be determined in advance. One color (a hue, or shades
nd tints of one hue) should dominate. In the arrangement above blue
was selected as the dominant color, with a touch of orange as a comple-
nentary contrast. Arrangement by Mrs. Esther Wheeler and Mrs. Charles
G. Scholz.*

I think that all beginners are inclined to crowd too much
into their arrangements; I know that some of them never get
over the habit. A good slogan is:

"When in doubt—leave it out!"

Just because a blossom, a bud, or a bit of foliage may be
beautiful in itself does not mean that adding it to your arrangement is going to make the latter more beautiful. Often
the effect is quite the contrary.

With scissors or snips poised for action, look over your nearly completed arrangement with a critical eye and a ruthless hand. Even though you may have done considerable cutting away and defoliating in preparing the material, chances are that a stray bit here and there can still come out to advantage. As you do this checking over, try to keep in mind all you have learned about design; as you proceed make a mental checkup on each point.

So much for the subtraction. Now as to the *addition*. Supplementing flowers or foliage to fill in gaps or holes, or to strengthen "lines," may be in order. A spray of foliage or a few flowers to break the sharp line of the container, if most of the plant material is placed above its rim, possibly will be just the finishing touch needed. But don't overdo it, and above all don't let this final filling in result in a confused, messy outline. Too much fussing at the last moment spoils many a good arrangement for both the show and the home.

WATER. If your plant material has been well hardened in advance, it will remain fresh and firm while you are putting the arrangement together, without any water in the container. Carry the completed job to the position it is to occupy, and fill the container, full, with cold water. If it's a home arrangement add fresh water at least daily—with heavy material and a shallow container replenishing may be needed even more frequently; you'll be surprised at the capacity a handful of cut flowers and a few husky leaves have for imbibing Adam's ale.

Final Check up

When your arrangement is completed, give it a final looking over to check it against all the things you should have kept in mind in designing and constructing it. As a memory freshener you can use the following scale of "points" to give yourself a score.

CHECK LIST

Design		30
Scale	10	
Balance	10	
Harmony	10	
Color		25
Harmony	15	
Placement	10	
(as affecting the design)		
Originality		25
Basic idea	15	
Distinction	10	
(in handling of material)		
Execution		20
Technical skill	15	
Condition of material	5	
		———
		100

NOTE: Compare this with the scoring system—which the judges would probably use in checking your exhibit at a flower show —on page 116.

*Arrangements by Mrs.
P. Joseph Leibrecht and
Mrs. Anne Elizabeth Er-
horn*

JUDGING

Design. *Look first
for the over-all effect
of the composition.
Is there evident a
planned, artistically
pleasing arrangement
of the material?*

Scale. *Are the plant
materials, the con-
tainer, and the acces-
sories well propor-
tioned? Here the small
figures—which carry
out the main line of
the arrangement—ex-
emplify good scale.*

CHAPTER IX

Judging Arrangements

The chances are that you do not aspire ever to become a judge of arrangements at flower shows. If that's the case, you demonstrate your wisdom, for there is no more thankless task under the horticultural sun. On the other hand, you do become, willy-nilly, a judge of your own work, and any information you can acquire concerning the judging of arrangements in general will help you immeasurably in constructive criticism of those you yourself attempt to create.

Of course we must have judges or we couldn't very well have competitive classes in flower arrangements at our shows, so you may sometime find yourself drafted for this ticklish job "for the good of the cause." Every year an army of serious-minded females gather up their notebooks and pencils, buy new dresses and hats, and flock to the "Judging Courses" that are now held in almost every state in the Union. Annually some eager aspirants temporarily forsake hubby and home, and for a day or two—or considerably more—sit through lecture after lecture and demonstration after demonstration, garnering information designed to help them with the final examination that (if they pass it) entitles them to be acclaimed to the world "accredited judges."

Anyone who plans seriously to take up judging should, if possible, attend a judges' course. In no other way, and from no other source, is it possible to get quite the same insight into the work which the judges at a show should accomplish—and good judging helps immensely in steadily raising the standards of our shows. This applies, of course, to horticulture as well as to arrangements. Fortunately the judges' courses are being carried out into smaller cities and rural communities, thus becoming available to many who formerly could not attend them.

A schedule of the Judging Course of the Federated Garden Clubs of New York State, which every year draws some five hundred applicants, from a score of states, may be of interest as indicating the subjects covered. Here is one:

A four-day Course presented by the New York Federation for the purpose of developing comprehensive judging of flower shows. Examination papers are marked and returned. *Only those taking the full four-day Course are eligible for the examination.*

The Federated Garden Clubs of New York State, Inc., will present Accredited Judges' Certificates to those who have cards showing they have passed five courses in New York State.

TUESDAY (10:00 A.M.) : A NEW APPROACH TO COLOR
by Miss Jacqueline Battersby

TUESDAY (1:30 P.M.) : TABLE TALKS AND TABLES
by The Following Outstanding Exhibitors
Mrs. Bernard Farley   *Mrs. James Earl Hathaway*
Mrs. John G. Hinman   *Mrs. John R. Lynch*
Miss Doris Naegeli   *Mrs. John H. Squires, Jr.*
Mrs. John C. Stark

TUESDAY (2:30 P.M.) : ROCK GARDENS
Their place in the garden design, planting, care and standards for judging
by T. H. Everett

WEDNESDAY (10:00 A.M.) : JUDGING THE HORTICULTURAL CLASSES OF FLOWERS
by Dr. R. C. Allen

WEDNESDAY (2:00 P.M.) : FLOWER ARRANGEMENT
The Oriental and Occidental Schools
Our Inheritance in a Pageant of the Periods
*by Mrs. Philip E. Erhorn, Mrs. Charles Hoffman,
Mrs. William G. Wheeler*

THURSDAY (10:00 A.M.) : FLOWER SHOW PRACTICE
by Mrs. Jules E. Rosenthal

THURSDAY (2 P.M.) : FLOWER ARRANGEMENT
The American School
Composition—Flower Arrangements and Accessories
by Mrs. Charles G. Scholz

FRIDAY (10:00 A.M.) :

Written Examination for those having attended all lectures of this course. No notes or books to be brought for reference during the examination.

The Reading Examination required for the National Council's Certificate will be given during this period to those having had three or more Judging Courses in any State.

FRIDAY (1:00 P.M.) :

Artistic Arrangement Show to be judged by those having attended all lectures.

Life Members have the privilege of attending all lectures but not the examinations.

Sustaining Members have the privilege of attending the complete Judges' Course including the examination.

Associate Members have the privilege of attending two lectures—one on Horticulture and one on Arrangement.

(From the schedule of the Fifteenth Course for Flower Show Exhibitors and Judges held at the Waldorf Astoria Hotel, New York City, January 21, 22, 23, 24, 1947.)

The Judge's Job

The job of a judge at a flower show is a combination of the specific and the nebulous—and therefore not an easy one. It is specific so far as the objective is concerned, but nebulous as to the means by which the objective is to be reached.

In each class under consideration the judge is supposed to select the best, and usually a second and third best—sometimes more. The rub is how the "best" is to be determined; and at this point (where more than one judge is concerned, as is usually the case) the matter of personal taste comes in.

Right here the judge should be careful to distinguish between personal taste and personal *prejudice*. For example, it is quite proper for a judge to express—and to defend—his or her opinion that the design in one arrangement is better than that in another; it is not proper to favor one arrangement over another because it happens to contain red flowers, whereas the judge, personally, intensely dislikes red. Nor should he rule against a line, as compared to a mass, arrangement because he likes his bouquets fat instead of skinny.

Another problem in selecting the "best" is to determine on what basis comparisons are to be made. This is especially important in cases where competition is close.

The National Council of State Garden Clubs has, as the result of many years of experience, worked out a scale of points to be used as a basis for judging "artistic-arrangement" classes. (This—or some similar—scale should be included in the printed flower-show schedule, but often is not.) If no such scale has been selected by the flower-show management, the judges should agree among themselves—before judging starts —as to what point system they will follow. Here is the National Council scale of points:

Color combination	25
Relation to container	10
Proportion and balance	25
Distinction and originality	20
Suitability of combination of materials	10
Condition	10
	100

(See also point scale on page 111.)

COLOR COMBINATION. In other words, *color harmony*. In allowing points for this, the judge should be a bit on guard. Color is likely to influence one's decisions to a degree even beyond the 25 points allotted to it. The judge should keep in mind that the scale reads "color *combination*," not just color alone. In classes which call for some particular emphasis on color (such as an analogous harmony, a triad, or "a monochromatic harmony in orange"), color should be examined much more critically than would otherwise be the case.

Arrangements by Mrs. Anne Elizabeth Erhorn and Mrs. James I. Coddington

JUDGING

Balance *is a matter of visual impression. Here the two solid figures "broaden the base," and keep the arrangement from appearing top-heavy.*

Focal point *should be sufficiently dominating to hold observer's attention. Main lines of design should lead to it.*

117

Here are two arrangements made with the same flowers. The one on the left is a fairly standardized symmetrical design. Rearranged, with slightly different container and base, it has infinitely more originality. The rather squatty, static effect has been changed to one of obvious dynamic rhythm.

RELATION TO CONTAINER. This is another way of expressing what in Chapter III (page 24) we discussed under the term "Harmony" (as distinct from *color* harmony). It includes consideration of the scale, color, texture, and general character of the plant material in relation to the container—a point frequently overlooked by judges.

PROPORTION AND BALANCE. In other words, the technical correctness of the design. Any good arrangement should pass on this score; an arrangement *not* possessing satisfactory proportion and balance should be scaled down sharply. "Proportion" has reference also to the scale of the arrangement as a whole to the space occupied. This space, in most instances, is predetermined by the show schedule.

DISTINCTION AND ORIGINALITY. These comprise the most difficult point to score—at least the one on which, when serving as judges ourselves, we have most frequently disagreed with our co-judges. On the National Council scale a maximum

*Here we start with a pair of accessories that suggest movement and call for
n arrangement that will carry out this theme. The standardized crescent
esign (left) fails to conform to this motif. Rearrangement (right), with one
rved spray of foliage added, brings unity and does the trick.*

of 20 points is allowed. This means that an arrangement
possessing distinction and originality may be off quite a few
points in other respects and still be a blue-ribbon winner. Yet
how frequently one sees top honors go to a composition that,
although technically good in other respects, cannot lay the
slightest claim to either distinction or originality.

These two attributes are not synonymous. There can be *distinction,* a certain "style" or "verve" in the way the material
is handled, with little or no originality in the design of the
composition; and *vice versa.* Distinction has more to do with
the *execution* of the composition; originality with the *conception* back of it. (For a further discussion of originality, see
pages 174 and 175.)

SUITABILITY OF COMBINATION OF MATERIALS. This, again, is
harmony or unity of the plant material—flowers, foliage, fruit,
pods, or what have you. Any disunity or lack of harmony here
certainly adversely affects the over-all charm of the composition
as a whole. Therefore, in judging, lack of "suitability" should
be scored down severely. Too often it is entirely overlooked.

CONDITION. This refers to the condition of the material. A merry war goes on between the flower art experts and the real dirt gardeners as to how much consideration, in judging arrangements, should be given to the condition of the plant material. The former maintain that a twisted, misshapen, or even diseased flower spray or branch may give just the needed line or color harmony, while the latter tear their hair in rage when a container full of perfectly grown Tulips or Roses is given the go-by in favor of a design worked out with some puny blossoms and dead twigs.

As is usual in such instances, the answer lies somewhere between the two extremes. *Horticultural perfection, as such, is entitled to no consideration in judging "artistic arrangements."* On the other hand, bug-eaten foliage and half-wilted blooms should be penalized, not because they are poor specimens horticulturally, but when, and if, they mar the artistic merit of the composition—and they usually do!

Another point that frequently arises in connection with "condition of material" is whether an arrangement should be judged "as is" when the judges come to it, or whether some allowance should be made for wilting (or, in some instances, opening) of flowers that may have taken place between the time the arrangement was made and the time it is judged.

As a rule, the wilting of plant material is directly the result of failure on the exhibitor's part properly to harden and condition it. Since this is his fault, the arrangement should be penalized accordingly. However, it sometimes happens—especially in local summer shows, or under extremely unfavorable conditions—that a delay in judging, a drafty location, or some other circumstance *not* the exhibitor's fault has been the cause of the trouble. Then very properly some allowance can be made.

JUDGING

Rhythm *adds grace and interest. Look for rhythm of form in curves and flowing lines; for color rhythm in the way colors blend into each other.*

Arrangement by Mrs. George A. Lofland

Unity *is to be found in a close relationship in form, color, texture, and spirit between plant material, container, and accessories.*

Arrangement by Mrs. Ralph Ferd

Judging Procedure

A few hints as to some other aspects of judging, quite aside from the proper "scoring" of exhibits, may not be amiss.

1. If you agree to serve as a judge, *get there on time*. Failure to do so indicates great inconsideration for a host of other folks: the show management, your fellow judges, and the crowd of show visitors who will be impatiently waiting for the judging to be finished.

2. Study the show schedule in advance and make yourself familiar with the sections and the classes—especially the classes you have been asked to judge. (Here is a sample schedule for arrangement classes):

FLOWER ARRANGEMENTS

A) Arrangement in any suitable container, Roses predominating.

B) Miniature arrangement in old-fashioned manner.

C) Non-competitive Class. Arrangement in pottery container featuring yellow flowers.

D) Class of Contrasts. Two arrangements in one space representing opposite ideas. (Example: Black and White, Hot and Cold, East and West, et cetera.)

E) Arrangement for summer terrace on an occasional table furnished by the exhibitor. Over all dimensions of the table not to exceed 24″ x 24″. Accessories permitted in this class.

F) Invitation Class. Arrangement in natural container. (Example: Gourds, shells, roots, wood, marble, et cetera.)

(NOTE: With the exception of Class E no accessories will be permitted. Arrangements will be placed on tables (no niches) against a neutral background. Size of space allowed for each exhibit is 32″ x 27″. Space allowed for miniature arrangements will be 12″ x 12″. No painted or shellacked materials will be allowed.)

3. In case any exhibit does not conform to the class in which it is entered, consult (with your co-judges) the schedule chairman before disqualifying it.

JUDGING

Color harmony *is important, but the judge should not allow it to blind him to other possible defects. The maximum number of points for color is 25.*

Arrangement by Mrs. Philip Ives

Originality. *The most rarely found of any of the qualities a judge looks for in flower arrangements. When it is present, it merits suitable recognition.*

Arrangement by Mrs. Norman R. Johnson

4. Don't waste time. Stick to the matter in hand; we have worked with many judges who actually consumed more time making suggestions how this, that, or the other arrangement *should* have been done than in selecting the winners from those before them.

5. *Eliminate*. Make a quick survey of all the entries in a class, and obliterate from consideration those that don't have a chance. This does away with confusing "going over," and leaves you free to concentrate on the winners.

6. Make up your own mind as to the first, second, and third winners *before* you consult with your co-judges; then discuss with them the merits and demerits of the candidates for consideration.

7. *Don't be a "hold-out."* Many arrangements are judged not by a team of judges (usually three) but by one member who absolutely refuses to give in to his or her co-workers on any point. It's all right to argue—but you should also co-operate: There are other classes waiting to be judged!

8. Remember that your decisions are the result of teamwork. If you are outvoted, accept it gracefully; and above all don't go round explaining to any exhibitor that *you* would have given her a prize but your co-judges didn't know enough to. (This has been done!)

9. Co-operate with the show management in respect to how "severe" the judging is to be. Many judges refuse to give a first to an arrangement that is not top notch, feeling that to do so would reflect on their own knowledge of what a good arrangement should be. This is not the case. One cannot expect to use the same standards in judging a long-established big city flower show and some local show that is struggling to establish itself, most of the exhibitors in which may have had little or no previous experience. Too harsh judging may discourage them from ever trying again.

Part Two

SPECIAL TYPES OF ARRANGEMENTS

Arrangement by Mrs. Alden D. Hart

AMARYLLIS, *supplemented by Aspidistra foliage, in an old candle mold—a happy solution of how to take care of thick, fleshy stems and make heavy blooms "face" as desired.*

CHAPTER X

Arrangements for the Home

It is all very well to tell the busy homemaker that she should take the time to make distinguished arrangements, but there are periods in our lives when all the waking time we have must be devoted to essentials. Nevertheless we want fresh flowers about us to ease the strain of too tense living. It is at such times that making very simple arrangements for the home becomes a necessity. But the simplest of arrangements are better than none, and in making them you will be doing the best you can under difficult circumstances to enliven the spirit of your living rooms. One such type of composition is the

One-flower Arrangement

When the Japanese speak of one-flower arrangements, they refer to compositions in which but a single blossom is used, with supplementary foliage. As we employ the term, it more often applies to arrangements in which several flowers of the same variety are grouped. Really distinguished compositions of this type can be made in much less time than it takes to put together an arrangement in which several different kinds of flowers are used.

(*Springtime note:* To provide for an abundance of such arrangements, and to have them above the average in quality, the arranger should plan in advance for materials with which to make them. In purchasing seeds, shrubs, and plants, keep this objective in mind.)

FOLIAGE. As most single-flower arrangements depend upon the foliage quite as much as upon the cut blooms for their effect, and as distinctive foliage is more likely to be lacking in the average garden than good blooms, give this special consideration. Magnolias, Laurel, Rhododendrons, Leucothoe, Pieris, and Wintergreen Barberry *(Berberis julianae)* provide season-long foliage material. Vines (perennial and annual), such as Wisteria and Bittersweet, supply graceful sprays for interesting line effects. Some annuals and perennials—Euphorbia and Globe-thistle *(Echinops ritro)*, for instance—have exceptionally decorative foliage.

PERENNIALS. In this group Peonies should perhaps come first. Select one or two singles and semi-doubles in addition to the doubles. One full-blown flower, a half-open bloom, a few buds in various stages of development, and some of the beautifully cut foliage of the plant itself can scarcely fail to produce a satisfactory arrangement. Hardy Chrysanthemums are the autumn mainstays. The large-flowered sorts are especially good for line arrangements, the smaller for massing.

Other perennials which are "naturals" for one-flower arrangements are Japanese or Siberian Iris with foliage, Chinese Delphinium, Oriental Poppies, with some of their exceptionally decorative tight buds and deeply cut foliage. Tritomas, with their own foliage or that of Calla, Ismene, or Aspidistra, are ideal for rooms in the modern manner.

Wildlings such as large Thistles, Waterlilies, Milkweed, Queen Anne's Lace, and Cat-tails enable the arranger to get out-of-the-ordinary effects.

BULBS. Most of the hardy bulbs, beginning with Hyacinths and Narcissus and passing on to Tulips, garden Lilies, and Lycoris, make excellent cut flowers. Tender bulbs and corms, such as Montbretias, Tuberous Begonias, Gladiolus, Ismenes, Callas, Amaryllis, and Crinums, are all worth while. With some, you'll need supplementary foliage, such as large-leaved Begonias, Monstera, or Birds-nest Fern.

Arrangement by Mrs. Lillian Norstad

MINIATURES. For "quickie" home arrangements, to add a spot of color here or there, try small arrangements of small flowers, such as the Floribunda Roses used here.

ANNUALS. The large-flowered annuals can be whipped up into a one-flower arrangement in no time. Double and ruffled Petunias with their sturdy stems and lush foliage are good. In cutting, select gracefully curving stems.

Large-flowered Zinnias or Marigolds make bold compositions. Dwarf varieties placed in pottery jugs, jars, or pitchers, or metal or wooden containers of peasant design can be used for informal tables and deep window sills.

Other satisfactory annuals for this purpose are Gaillardias, Calendulas, China Asters, and Moonflowers—the latter for "floating" table arrangements.

FLORISTS' MATERIAL, such as Gardenias, Camellias, and hot-house Chrysanthemums are easy to arrange alone. Use very few flowers as the focal center of the composition, and as a foil and to give height and breadth employ branches of Rhododendron, Magnolia, Kalmia, or other bold, dark foliage.

In making arrangements of flowers of a single species or variety there is always a great temptation to use too many blooms. If flowers are purchased from a florist, there usually is the additional problem of having them all the same size and about equally opened up. Perhaps the day will come when commercial florists will carry, for the benefit of the discriminating, a few buds or half-opened blooms.

In cutting one's own flowers from garden or greenhouse, however, it is possible to obtain some variety in this respect, and usually to get also a few curved or crooked stems. These will prove of great help in getting an artistic effect, as may be seen by a glance at the arrangements shown on pages 83, 89, 198, and 258.

Extreme simplicity marks these arrangements, and yet there is no sense of monotony—no feeling that the addition of flowers of some other kind would have added to their attractiveness. The candle-mold container in the arrangement by Mrs. Alden de Hart (page 126) is just about ideal for rendering less conspicuous the fleshy and rather ungraceful stems of the Amaryllis, while at the same time making it possible to space

Arrangement by Mrs. Austin S. Phillips

SIMPLICITY ITSELF—this arrangement of Tulips and Apple blossoms! Yet what could bring a more cheerful breath of spring into the house? A bold silhouette, well suited for a window sill.

the blooms so that each one shows up clearly. The curved Aspidistra leaves provide rhythm and motion to what would otherwise be an unpleasantly stiff and static design.

In a vase of Zinnias (page 289) the same effect is obtained by the use of tapering sprays of foliage, with a few leaves so placed as to break the hard, straight lines which are characteristic of the container.

In each the *design,* though extremely simple, gives evidence of having been carefully thought out. They are studied, but not *too* studied.

The individual flowers, while large, remain in *scale* with the containers because so few of them are used. The use of a half dozen or more fully opened blooms of either the Amaryllis or the Zinnias would have thrown them out of scale.

BALANCE—in both these examples asymmetrical balance—has been nicely handled. In your mind's eye project a vertical line through the center of either arrangement, and see how the flowers and foliage on each side of it equalize each other even though they are not at all similar in their arrangement.

In each case, too, the over-all effect is one of *harmony.* This, of course, is much more readily attained when only one or two kinds of plant material are used (as in these arrangements) than when a number of different flowers or types of foliage is employed. Nevertheless these same arrangements in other containers—such as elaborate cut glass or polished silver—would lack the harmony they now possess. A feeling that something was out of tune would result, even though the observer might not realize just what it was or why it caused the impression.

Other Simple Designs

Another easy way to arrange flowers for the home in a hurry is to make mixed bouquets. Go out into the garden and cut the best of whatever you find in bloom. Blend these in vases or bowls, grouping harmonious colors. Sometimes it's fun to see how many flowers can be successfully used in one arrangement.

Arrangement by Mrs. Louise Hoffman

ROSES, with their own foliage, are ideal for "one-flower" arrangements. A bit more classy than most garden flowers, they keep company with silver and glass rather than earthenware or pewter.

Among my favorite combinations is one of pink, blue, white, and violet. For height I use *Salvia farinacea,* Heuchera, or Astilbe Fanal; for focal interest and side lines, garden Roses; "fillers" are violet and pink Verbenas, Dianthus, Violas, and Pansies, Scabiosa, Salpiglossis, Petunias, Centaurea, Stokesia,

Arrangement by Mrs. G. F. Roberts

SIMPLICITY-PLUS: *Gladiolus are conceded to be "difficult" flowers to arrange. Too often they are placed in large vases or baskets with stems of equal length in a monotonous fanlike design. Here a few spikes have been well chosen for line and weight. Foliage and buds give height and breadth while the perfection of the fully opened florets rounds out the composition.*

Arrangement by Mrs. Frank C. Boes

SPIRIT OF SPRING: *Branches starred with bloom
are combined with Tulips, Jack-in-the-pulpit, and Lily-
of-the-valley in a bouquet which breathes the spirit of
spring. This is not a perfectly executed design, but its
free simplicity suggests the sort of thing that is appropriate for use in the home. The creation of an
arrangement of this type requires only a reasonable
amount of time and thought.*

135

Arrangement by Mrs. C. W. Zimmerer

FOR A GUEST ROOM: Here's a happy gesture of welcome to a visitor. Once you get the knack of it, arrangements like this can be made in a few minutes—and they do make a difference in the atmosphere of a room.

Catananche, or—late in the season—small hardy Chrysanthemums.

Orange-red-and-gold compositions can be made with Snapdragons, hardy Chrysanthemums, Marigolds, Rudbeckias, Calendulas, and yellow or orange Cosmos.

Tall, gracefully slender vases of Cosmos, China Asters, and Scabiosa, or Blue Lace Flowers are restful to the eye.

Tuzzy-muzzys, too, are easy and attractive for side tables, dressing rooms, and guestroom bedside tables. These fragrant miniatures, placed in an old-fashioned "hand" vase, may contain Dianthus, tiny Roses, Violas, Lavender, Myosotis, blooming Thyme, American Pineapple Mint, Lemon Verbena, Rose Geranium, and Rosemary.

CHAPTER XI

Arrangements for the Show

BY ANNE ELIZABETH ERHORN

So you've decided to try an "arrangement" for your local flower show! Perhaps, if you've never exhibited before, there are certain matters in connection with the undertaking that you wish you knew more about. Perhaps, even if you have exhibited before, there are things that, to your own detriment, you have overlooked. Let's discuss the situation.

The very first job of a would-be competitor in a flower show is to read the schedule! Then reread it until you are certain you understand it fully, in every detail. The finest arrangement, if it fails to "follow the schedule," will be disbarred even from being judged—let alone winning a prize.

As you go over the schedule, check the classes that you might be interested in. Then study them carefully until you have a clear understanding of each. If there is any question about what materials can be used or how the definition of the class is to be "interpreted," don't guess—*call the arrangement schedule chairman and find out.*

The judges, too, will have studied the schedule and will assume that the exhibitor has done the same. When judging an exhibit they will expect to find that:

1. The exhibitor has complied with the rules of the schedule in every detail.

2. The arrangement is in good proportion to the allotted space.

3. It has good design.

4. It has good color harmony.

5. The arrangement shows good technique in the way it is assembled.

6. The plant material is in good condition.

7. It has distinction and originality.

Having all this information clearly in mind, you will be able to determine the equipment necessary to meet successfully the requirements of the class you plan to enter. Then ask yourself these three questions:

1. Have I the right containers, accessories, and fabrics (if required) to use in this class?

2. Can I procure the plant material called for?

3. Am I capable of creditably interpreting the class in every detail?

If you have any doubt in your mind as to your ability to fill the requirements of the schedule, do not enter the class. This will save you much apprehension and disappointment on the day of the show. If, however, you decide that you can get together an ensemble which in all particulars meets the demands of the schedule, then by all means enter the class because, having spent the time necessary to make this decision, it is more than likely that you are proficient enough to create a worth-while picture which will prove to be an asset to your flower show, even if it does not win you a blue ribbon.

Having decided on the container, accessory, fabric, and plant materials—all of which must be harmonious in color and texture—you will next work out the details of your arrangement. If the class stresses *color,* concentrate on how you will use it—whether you wish to create a subtle picture in quiet tones or one with a dramatic, glorious blaze of color. Only after you have decided your color scheme will you give thought to design and other details.

If, on the other hand, the call is for *line,* concentrate on design, and obtain plant material best suited to create line, leaving color as secondary.

FOR
FLOWER SHOWS

*Arrangements by Mrs.
Rose Both and Mrs.
Bernard E. Farley*

Spring: *In show
work, schedules must
be followed meticu-
lously. Here the
"theme" called for was
"spring."*

Vegetables and
fruits: *Sounds like an
unexciting class, but
here the use of unusual
material, well ar-
ranged, drew a first
prize.*

Should the class call for a period arrangement, stress this in detail all through your composition, using only plant material and accessories that are typical of the era called for—Colonial, French, Victorian, or whatever it is.

Correct Scale

The size of the space allotted for the display of your arrangement is also of great importance. Your schedule will give this—but don't trust to your imagination in trying to visualize it. Cut out a piece of paper or cardboard to the size of your background (the height and width of the niche) and fasten this with thumbtacks to a wall over a worktable. Put another paper or cardboard the size of your "floor" space (the horizontal dimensions of the niche or the space assigned) on the table below this background.

Next choose a container that will fill the space adequately. It should be neither too large nor too small. I have found that a fairly satisfactory rule, if you use a tall container, is to have it slightly over one third the height of the space. For instance: in the Calla arrangement illustrated (page 103), my vase and stands—stands are counted as part of your container—measure sixteen inches in height, and the space was forty-five inches high. If a low container is used, the same rule would apply to the *width* of the container in relation to the height of background.

If a large container has been used, and you have chosen large flower and leaf forms for your arrangement, do not use a dainty, inadequate accessory; use one of suitable size and weight for your composition. If you do not possess an acceptable accessory and cannot procure one, do not enter the class. Many ribbons are lost as a result of the use of unsuitable accessories.

Public Appeal

When planning an arrangement for a flower show, always remember that it must possess public appeal. To attain this,

Arrangement by Mrs. Claire Stickles

VEGETABLES AND FRUITS are often called for in flower-show schedules. This colorful composition includes Tomatoes, Beans, Beets, and Peas, with foliage of Mint, Leeks, and Cos Lettuce. Eggplant, Squash, Okra, French Artichokes offer especially interesting forms and colors.

you must create a picture that will arrest attention either by its subtlety, originality, beauty of design, or color harmony. Have a reason for your arrangement, and make your reason apparent.

In making the arrangement illustrated (page 103) my idea was to create a flower picture for a modern home. I visualized a room with a wall of glass brick, furnished with sophisticated simplicity, its color scheme a soft, cool green. In considering what type of arrangement I could make for such a room, I realized that if I introduced brilliant color, it would bring a disturbing note into the tranquil atmosphere of the room, so I decided to use Callas, which, because of their classic simplicity of form, will always have a place in modern design.

I arranged the Callas very simply, with their own foliage, in a lovely modern clear green glass container, which I stood on a glass brick, with a black wooden block underneath. I then placed the finished arrangement (in my imagination) on a table in front of the glass wall, through which the sun was brightly shining, adding a note that further emphasized the serenity of the room. In staging this arrangement in the niche supplied me, I placed in the back of it a low-wattage electric-light bulb to simulate the light from the glass wall and the sunshine.

Preshow Rehearsal

In a flower show never use plant material with which you are unfamiliar, or you may be disappointed. Some flower and leaf forms are difficult to use; others do not lend themselves to design, while some do not stand up well in arrangements. Always use a container that will hold sufficient water to nourish the number of flowers used in your arrangement. There is no excuse for wilted plant material in a flower show, and nothing is more disappointing to the public than to view a prize-winning exhibit that is wilting by the time they see it.

To assure yourself that you will not err in this respect, you should stage a full-dress rehearsal a day or two before the flower show. Assemble your container, accessories, fabrics, and such plant materials as you have to use. Then build your arrangement just as you have planned it for the show.

When you are satisfied that your composition has good proportion and balance, is harmonious in color, and creates a picture that pleases you, place it in a room of comfortably warm temperature and let it remain there for at least the same length of time that it would be on exhibition at the flower show. This test will enable you to assure yourself of the lasting qualities of the chosen plant materials and allow you time to make any necessary substitutions.

Procuring and Keeping Materials

Always purchase or cut plant materials the day before the show, and season by immersing in deep water for several hours. If material is to be cut from your own garden, take a pail of water out with you, cut stems at a slanting angle, and plunge them immediately deeply into the water. This will be of great help in preserving the pristine freshness of the flowers.

Strip off all unnecessary foliage. No foliage should be left on stems that are under water. There are two reasons for this: if foliage is stripped from flower stems, the water will not foul so quickly; and if container has a small opening, stripped stems take up less room.

Many plant materials need special treatment. For instance, Dahlias should have their stems seared or plunged in a few inches of hot water for several minutes; Poppy and Peony stems should be seared; those of Lilac and all flowering shrubs should be split or crushed; stems of Stocks should be crushed or scraped. Calla-lilies are long lasting, but their green leaves wilt easily. To prevent the wilting of Calla and similar "soft" leaves, completely immerse them in cold water for several hours before using, then they will last as long as the flowers.

When choosing foliage of any kind, avoid cutting very new leaves or shoots, as they are delicate and wilt quickly. Choose rather those that have been open for a day or two; they are hardened and will last longer.

Preparing Materials in Advance

Since exhibitors in most shows are now officially permitted to use wire as an aid in the building of arrangements—if it is done expertly and is not visible to the observer—I find that this is of great assistance in shaping leaves to create definite "line" designs. (See page 105.)

Illustrated is one manner in which this is accomplished. This work may be done at home, and, if so, will prove to be a great time-saver. If you have your stems cut to size, all foliage selected and wired, the flowers for each arrangement in separate bunches (with extras for emergencies), it is a simple thing to assemble your arrangements on your arrival at the show. In fact, you may even prearrange your flowers, or many of them, at home, fasten them together with Scotch tape, and have only to secure them in your vase on a pinholder. Or, as in the Calla arrangement shown—which is in a glass container, where one may not use a holder—secure it with Scotch tape, taking care to hold the arrangement in a good position while making it secure.

Equipment Needed

Before leaving home, check to see if you have all the necessary equipment needed for your exhibits: holders, wire, scissors, Scotch tape, florists' picks, stands, fabrics, accessories, containers, and your plant materials.

Be sure to leave home in good time, and arrive early. When your arrangement is completed, leave the show floor as soon as possible, as this is of great assistance to the show committee, and appreciated by the judges, who, on their arrival, like to find the show ready for judging.

CHAPTER XII

Line Arrangements

BY ESTHER G. WHEELER

Floral compositions of the type usually described as "line arrangements" may be put in two main categories: (1) those of the still-life sort, which may be beautiful in many respects, but which have a "dead-pan" effect; and (2) those which express motion, symbolic of activity and life. We see too many of the former in the flower shows of today and too few of the latter, which may be attributed to overzealous schedule preparers. Our concern here is with the second class—the "vibrant" arrangements.

A flower arrangement, to be really good, must be alive and must express motion—what painters call the "spirit of the picture." Naturally it must have beauty *and* grace; the achievement of this end will depend entirely upon the ability of the arranger. A good flower arranger must possess some knowledge of horticulture, must have confidence and command of the material used. But possession of these attributes is only the beginning. The next step is to turn these attainments to artistic purposes. Thereafter the quality of the arrangement will be in direct proportion to the ability of the arranger.

A good arrangement cannot be made without grace. One does not get grace from books and studies; it is an art which is inherent in the material. Yet grace in some measure may be achieved by the handling of flowing, gliding outlines of the material, augmented with related parts, so adjusted that the whole becomes a finished picture, retaining a "feeling of motion" throughout.

DePiles, in his *Lives of the Painters,* says "that a painter can only have it (grace) from nature, and doth not know that he hath it, nor in what degree, nor how he communicates it to his works: and that grace and beauty are two different things; beauty pleases by rules, and grace without them."

Perhaps there are too many flower arrangers who "just arrange" and too few of those who, like DePiles's painter, "doth not know that he hath it." Perhaps one should not criticize too severely or condemn rules just because niches at our flower shows are filled with abundant and conglomerate mass arrangements, confined in small areas and without line. But when one bears in mind that the old masters are not devoid of line and that flower arrangements are supposed to be pictures —one wonders!

Motion can be effected by repetition, or by a succession of lines simulating waves; by the blending of color, such as monochromatic and analogous color schemes; by the gradation of forms, such as the use of buds, half-opened and fully opened flowers; and by weight contrasts. Nevertheless it is the use of the *rhythmic line* that produces most of the blue-ribbon winners in our shows.

The *Hogarth curve,* that languorous serpentine line forming a lazy S, has become the symbol of the American art of flower arranging. It was publicized by the English artist Hogarth more than two hundred years ago and termed by him the Line of Beauty. Hogarth's line has extraordinary grace and movement, and is particularly adapted to upright arrangements. It may be used in any of its seven gradations in either the upright or the horizontal compositions. This line superimposes *grace* on beauty.

Arrangement by Mrs. Audrey H. Dunn

PURE LINE: A first-prize line arrangement of dried twigs and Orchids. Looks easy, doesn't it? Just wait till you try it yourself!

147

The spiral, frequently found in nature, is a fundamental component of natural beauty. The compact unit of the Pine cone, simple flowers with rows of florets going round and round like a spiral, or vines and tendrils resembling coiled rope, are excellent examples of this line. It is seldom used, but, when it is, it is dynamic and has telling effect upon the observer.

The simple vertical line may become rhythmic by accentuating its height to give an ascending feeling. It then becomes majestic and seems to carry motion to higher levels. It has great dignity and solemnity, yet it is an easy line for the amateur to use.

The horizontal line induces a feeling of slow or reserved motion, giving a sense of tranquillity. The Hogarth line may be used in variety here and may be joined or used in

contrasting curves, presenting not only an ornamental but a pleasing aspect.

The diagonal line, unless supported by other lines, suggests a leaning-tower instability; is seldom used in flower arrangements. We find this line in the diagonal opening of the conch shell. It may be used to depict some idea called for by exotic flower-show schedules.

Arrangement by Mrs. Jesse Thomas Fort

ONE-FLOWER LINE: A typical composition of the modern modified Japanese type. "Heaven," "Man," and "Earth" are there, but the material is handled more freely and informally.

The circle is a rhythmic line, truly satisfying to the eye because it returns to itself; but it may not be interesting unless other lines are introduced to give variety, or the "rounds" accentuated by using round containers, rounded plant material, and round stands.

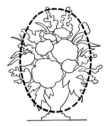

The oval, because of its variety plus simplicity, is as much favored as the circle. When the oval has a little more of the cone added to it (as in the egg), it becomes distinctly a combination of the two. The Pineapple is of this shape. It may be used to good advantage in contrast.

The crescent of the new moon is considered the most beautiful form in nature. Its line suggests slow rhythmic motion and in American arrangements is next in popularity to the Hogarth line.

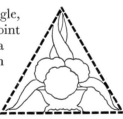

Should one wish to express the bizarre or a restless motion, a sharper Hogarth line, such as a zigzag, may give an exciting effect. (See illustration, page 151.)

The pyramid, or symmetrical triangle, with its diminishing line from base to point and gradually lessening to its center, is a beautifully balanced form, and is much used for modern mass arrangements. It is, however, a form rather than a line.

LINE
ARRANGEMENTS

*Arrangements by Mrs.
Otto Langhans and Mrs.
Grace R. Leibel*

Line arrangements
*have the emphasis
placed on design
(usually a sharp sil-
houette) but in the
modern form no
longer follow the
strict, formalized
rules of Japanese
flower art. Each
flower, leaf, or
branch, however,
should stand out
very clearly.*

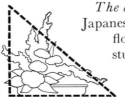

The asymmetrical triangle, as developed by the Japanese, is considered the most perfect form for flower arrangement. Through centuries of study the Japanese evolved definite rules whereby art and nature are blended, with its principles based on the universal fundamentals of design. The asymmetrical triangle is symbolic. It represents Heaven, Man, and Earth, and is founded on the Confucian teaching that man identifies himself with both heaven and earth. Its fundamental idea is the suggestion, not only of the living plant, but its surroundings and the conditions under which it grows. When it is used for arrangements in the oriental manner, it achieves balance by keeping the tip of the tallest spray over its base. This line may sway away, but it must return at its highest point.

In the Japanese triangle proportion is achieved by cutting the primary line one and a half to twice the height of the container (or length, if container is flat), depending on the visual weight, color, and texture of the container. The secondary line is then cut two thirds the height of the main line and tipped away at an angle of about 30° from the primary line. The third line is cut about one third the length of the primary line and tipped forward at an angle of about 45°. This makes the asymmetrical triangle three dimensional, giving it a foreground, a middle ground, and a background, so that one gets the impression of looking into the arrangement instead of at it. Thus we get height, width, and depth.

The Japanese triangle is rhythmic. Its slow, subtle curves turn inward gracefully in rhythmic lines. It has stability, which is achieved by having strong lines at the base of the arrangement and by keeping the stems together for about four inches above the base. This gives the finished arrangement the appearance of growing directly out of the container, or rising like a tree from the ground. It has unity, as interpreted by nature.

Only plants are used which grow naturally together, in the same environment and at the same time, above, below, or on the level with each other. While the modern form, or Moribana (Mori, meaning shaped up; bana, flowers), uses flowers more profusely, the great linear beauty of the asymmetrical triangle is not lost, nor is the natural growth of the plant material distorted.

The creation of a good arrangement of flowers, based on the fundamental principles of design, blended with nature's rhythmic line and grace, can be an experience as enriching and satisfying as that of painting a fine picture.

MASS ARRANGEMENTS

Arrangements by Mrs. Kimball Prince and Mrs. Louise Hoffman

Mass arrangements *in the modern manner are less densely crowded than in former days, more informal, and often reveal a more or less decided line design despite the crowding together of the flowers.*

CHAPTER XIII

Mass Arrangements

BY BARBARA BECK

I like flowers, *masses* of flowers. I need them to live with indoors as well as out. Not for me, by choice, the delicate line of an oriental arrangement or the muted coloring of a monochrome. Give me flowers that, when one enters a room, really speak out a welcome of good cheer that can't be missed or misunderstood.

From all of which it may be gathered that I like mass arrangements. In England, where I grew up, we used flowers in masses to decorate home interiors. There were seldom "arrangements" in the modern sense of the word, not even Victorian arrangements; just masses of flowers, often of only one kind, huge bowls of Wallflowers or of red Roses, towering spikes of Delphiniums; Sweet Peas, Lupines—whatever happened to be in season. But these floral decorations dominated the space around them, keynoted the atmospheres of entire rooms, and big rooms at that.

Here in America we are not yet nearly so flower conscious as are our friends in England or in Europe. Despite the wonderful work that garden clubs have done here, we must admit that flowers, cut flowers in particular, are not so commonplace and intimate a part of our daily living. This is partly because flowers here are so much more expensive. In France, the woman who goes shopping for food adds, as a matter of course, some flowers to take home with it; flowers and perfume are almost as essential to her as bread.

Modern Mass Arrangements

The differences between mass arrangements of former times and those of today have been described and illustrated elsewhere in this volume, so I will not dwell upon them. The word "mass" in itself implies collecting, bringing together, forming in compact bodies; and so the term mass arrangements very naturally came to be applied to such floral bouquets as are shown in Flemish and Dutch paintings of the seventeenth and eighteenth centuries; modern mass arrangements resemble these old masterpieces in that they are composed of a considerable quantity of blooms, usually several species, crowded closely together in substantial containers.

One of the characteristics of contemporary mass arrangements, as compared to period arrangements, is that there is more definite planning in the use or distribution of color—the *color* design as distinct from the general design of the composition. Color harmonies in period designs are likely to be polychromatic—many colors used together—whereas in modern arrangements there more often is a definite analogous or complementary color scheme.

Following the introduction of Japanese flower art to American garden circles, and the period when it was more or less slavishly followed, there was a decided turn to "line" arrangements. I believe that the pendulum is now swinging back, that we are seeing, and will see, more good, full-bodied mass arrangements. Certainly mass arrangements are better suited to many of our present-day interiors that show colonial or Victorian influence.

I believe, too—and this conclusion is based on long experience—that flowers, even if crammed together in a mass arrangement, *last longer in good condition* than those separated in scanty line designs. Don't ask me the reason; but perhaps the fact that they help protect each other from drafts of air and from rapid transpiration may have something to do with it.

Arrangement by Mrs. L. N. Wilson, Mrs. Robert D. Veghte, and Mrs. Constance B. Wallace

COLOR RHYTHM, built into this modern mass design by the distribution of the color areas, is in marked contrast to the more or less haphazard placement of color in older types of mass arrangement.

First—the Color Scheme

When I set out to make a mass arrangement, either for a room in my home, a lecture, or a flower show, my first concern is the color scheme. Usually this is determined by the material at hand, or in season. If one flower—Peonies, Roses, Iris, for instance—is to dominate the arrangement, that sets the keynote; others are selected for their relationship to it; harmony or contrast as one decides. If you want an arrangement with real punch, avoid using too many colors no matter how well they may harmonize. And use big, bold blooms, or (if you must) closely knit groups of identical small ones, for the points of emphasis in your design.

Every arranger gradually acquires a list of flowers with which she likes to work. If she's a gardener, too (as she should be!), she can grow her favorites. Here are some that I like:

For Height. The delicate spires of Astilbe in white, pink, or red (variety Fanal) give feathery grace. Yellow Mimosa has a willowy softness. For dignified spikes I choose Delphiniums (Larkspur), the pristine whiteness or swooning pastel shades of Stocks, or the sturdy beauty of Antirrhinums or of Lupines.

Lilacs can be placed for either height or accent. That is true of other flowers too. For instance, the buds of Calla-lilies, Siberian Iris, Roses, and spring-flowering bulbs can be used with, or instead of, flower spikes to provide the desired height.

For smaller mass arrangements, height may be given with *Salvia farinacea, Lavendula vera,* Veronica, Cynoglossum, Lythrum, or Achillea. And there are always spring-flowering shrub sprays, especially fine with Tulips and other spring bulbs.

For Emphasis. For massed effects the big buxom flowers are easy to arrange and breath-taking in their beauty. The list of possibilities is long. In one group we may put Peonies, garden Roses, Dahlias, large Chrysanthemums, Oriental Poppies, Marigolds, Zinnias, Calendulas, and China Asters. These are the big round forms, each of which makes a natural center of interest to the eye.

Even more distinguished are members of the Lily family and allied species: all the garden Lilies, Amaryllis, Callas, Lycoris, Hyacinths, Tulips, and Daffodils. From the greenhouse or in the South we can use such exotics as Passion Flowers, Camellias, and Orchids.

Still another possibility is in massed groups of smaller blooms like Violets, Cinerarias, or even Geraniums. Try a large pewter container with a mass of red Geraniums for a room with little sunlight. Their cheerful, homely beauty is good to look at and to live with.

FILLERS. Flowers less emphatic than those we have just been discussing, yet lovely massed alone and natural for mixed mass arrangements, include Bulbous Iris, Narcissi, minor spring bulbs such as Leucocoryne, Freesias, Ixias, Bouvardia, and Lily-of-the-valley. Pansies come into this class, too, as do Carnations, Sweet Peas, small-flowered hardy Chrysanthemums, and garden flowers like Pyrethrum, Centaureas, and Stokesias.

The idea is to have flowers always at hand that can be arranged quickly but effectively. If particular care is taken in the selection of the vase, many of the flowers mentioned in the preceding paragraphs need very little "arranging" to create a beautiful picture. In the spring, if you have Lily-of-the-valley, just gather a bowlful and enjoy them. Their fragrance will follow you all through the house. I do not see how anyone can be without flowers indoors—masses of beauty and fragrance to rest the eyes and lift the spirit.

Sometimes the color scheme may take its origin from the container. This is likely to be the case when you have begged, borrowed, bought, or stolen a container for a show exhibit, and will be buying your plant material. In any case there should definitely be appropriate harmony between the material and the container. (See, for instance, the illustrations on pages 15 and 89.)

Construction

In putting together a mass arrangement I employ no special technique or "tricks" other than those familiar to most arrangers. One thing I do take particular care about is to make certain that the first element of the arrangement to be put in place is made firm as a rock. Usually this is the tallest flower (or group of flowers) or branch of foliage. It must be capable of anchoring the other material later built in around it. The arrangement may be begun with the focal point, or the dominant color accent, rather than the tallest material; but in any case let the start be a firm one.

Placement and Care

If flower arranging has any excuse for claiming a place as an art, its aim is to glorify the home and add to the joy of living, to serve as a tonic to the weary soul. Put your arrangements where they will dominate your rooms. Let flowers be part of your life!

If you make colorful mass arrangements you won't have to worry about backgrounds. They can stand on their own feet, as it were; they won't be "lost" if they are not silhouetted against a neutral background. Have them well lighted; use a suitable drape if conditions seem to call for it, and let them speak for themselves.

One thing more. I find I can keep my arrangements fresh considerably longer by the following simple expedients. I place several lumps of charcoal in the bottom of the container; I keep arrangements *out of drafts,* and (especially in winter) in a cool place at night; and I change the water *daily.* This can be done without disturbing the arrangement by setting the container in a pan or deep dish and running fresh water into the container from a pitcher or a small hose until it has overflowed for several minutes. Surplus water can then be syphoned out, down to the desired level. Try it and see how much longer your arrangements last!

CHAPTER XIV

Period Arrangements

BY LOUISE HOFFMAN

Many flower-show schedules call for arrangements done in a certain manner—"Victorian," "Colonial," "French," "Flemish"—and known, in general, as Period Arrangements. To the novice such categories frequently are confusing. Lack of a definite understanding results in exhibits that do not conform to the requirements, and for that reason never have a chance at winning a prize. An old Victorian container, dug out of the attic, does not in itself make a Victorian arrangement; any more than Parrot Tulips, a patched-up bird's nest (with the wrong kind of eggs in it), and a moth-eaten butterfly necessarily make a Flemish period composition.

When we study the development of the art of flower arrangement in the United States, it is interesting to trace the influence of the Occident on the one hand and the Orient on the other. These influences have created a happy "blend" easily recognized as a typically American flower arrangement. This kind of arrangement reflects an understanding of design. Color is used boldly or with subtlety—depending on the setting. Textures are carefully combined. Often these arrangements are highly "stylized." Many inexperienced flower arrangers do not understand the whys and wherefors for such arrangements—some actively dislike them.

There was a time, not so long ago, when it was perfectly satisfactory for most people to place cut flowers—usually masses of them—in vases or bowls in their houses, regardless of the so-called period. There was always the lady who had a "way" with flowers. She naturally enjoyed working with flowers. She arranged them so that each flower appeared at its best. She couldn't bear to crowd them too much. It seems quite logical to assume that this "lady with a way with flowers" is now leading the way in flower-arrangement demonstrations for our American homes.

When the Garden Club movement began some thirty years ago, flower shows followed naturally. A new field for study was opened when all sorts of classes for artistic arrangements were found in the flower-show schedules. Some of the early interpretations seem incredible to us today. Women learned that the Orientals had studied and practiced flower arrangements for centuries. They learned that the Japanese style was the most perfected style of all. So Japanese teachers and textbooks became popular here. Most Americans found that copies of purely Japanese arrangements were disappointing when placed in their own homes. But they learned to appreciate the beauty of line and restraint and the principles involved in creating a design. This knowledge intensified the interest when the urge came to do something about flowers in "period" settings.

Period arrangements are characterized by "mass" and "color" and belong to a certain era in Western or European history. The following periods may influence an American home: Classical, Medieval, Renaissance, Flemish, Italian, French (Neo-Classical), Georgian, Victorian (early, mid, and late), and Modern. The style of these periods is expressed through their great paintings, sculpture, architecture, ceramics, music, and literature. By studying these and selecting our housefurnishing accordingly, if we want "pure period," the style of flower arrangements is governed by the chosen period. Or if we prefer to blend or skillfully combine the furnishings of more than one period—as more and more people are doing today—we really create something more individual. After all, we can visit our museums to enjoy the art of the past. It seems more progressive and exciting to create something new rather than to try to copy the old.

Arrangement by Mrs. Charles C. Whitlock

MODIFIED FRENCH: *Suggestive of French period pieces, in its airily massed and gracefully arranged gay spring blooms, this composition is a bit free and unconventional to qualify as strictly "period."*

This is particularly true of period flower arrangements. If we copied the earliest examples as shown in the great paintings, they would be merely flowers used as a part of some larger composition. We want flower arrangements that are beautiful and complete "on their own" if necessary. So, with our knowledge of design learned from the Orientals, we add color and an abundance of plant material which our country produces.

To create something new we must first have an understanding of the old. The following periods are recognized by certain accepted definitions:

The *Classical* refers to Greek art, which was the first to realize the idea of beauty. Simplicity, usually expressed in perfection of symmetry of form, comes to mind. Greek Classic art became the greatest influence in Europe and America. One can visualize a beautiful white Grecian urn as an ideal container for certain kinds of flowers. White Lilies arranged formally, or in the symmetrical triangle form, can be accented by buds at the points of the triangle, with small palm leaves on each side at the neck of the container acting as a refined finish to the design. This example of the Classical could well be used in our modern homes. Naturally, it could be carried out in one color or a combination of colors as well. It is a basic form or design which may be worked out simply with garden flowers or more elaborately for special occasions and special settings.

The *Medieval* period is felt mostly in cathedrals and churches. Here flower arrangements are rightly blended with and subordinated to the appointments of the church. It is a field that requires the study and understanding of many church rituals and customs.

The *Renaissance* (Rebirth) period began in Italy in the thirteenth century, reached its climax in the fifteenth and sixteenth centuries, and affected art expression all over Europe. For the purposes of Renaissance period arrangements containers of bronze, marble, or heavy old Venetian glass may be used. The color should be warm generally—with cool accents of blues and greens. Tropical fruit forms are much used and may be combined with suitable flowers. The impression of richness of fabrics and flowers and fruits should be created. This is the period when the *individual* became important.

The *Italian* Renaissance of the sixteenth century, typified by Titian and Tintorello, taught us much of the use of rich brocades and velvets, fruits, glamorous garden backgrounds or canopied interiors, jewels and shining armor.

The *Flemish* period, because of the elaborate flower prints which are available for study, is better known to us. Realism was practiced. All obtainable flower forms were combined and placed in a variety of containers, usually bronze or bright metal urns. Often the flowers almost concealed the container. Accessories consisting of butterflies, birds' nests with eggs, and the like, added to the profusion expressed in the mass arrangements. It is not necessary to enumerate the many kinds of flowers used. Only those who wish to reproduce authentic period arrangements, as specified in a show schedule, would be interested. Also, the cost of material would be higher than for most period arrangements. If the home atmosphere is such that an arrangement "in the Flemish manner" would enhance it for a special occasion, a profuse, rich, colorful mass arrangement of suitable garden flowers, supplemented (if necessary) by the local florist's more unusual flowers, might be quite worth while.

A *French*-period arrangement is more formal, more delicate and subtle in color and more restrained in form than the Flemish. Fine porcelain urns (Sèvres or Meissen), the more classical alabaster vases, also delicate bronze containers are suitable. The finer, more delicate flowers are combined to suit the style of containers. For the home, the month of May, when French Lilacs are at their best, is the ideal time to "let yourself go" with this kind of arrangement. Lilacs and Tulips with other flowers can produce an entrancing French arrangement. It is also suitably fragrant. Of course Roses and Delphinium, with certain varieties of Clematis, also combine most elegantly.

The so-called *Colonial* type of arrangement can easily be adapted from the French period. We think of both as being done in pastels rather than bright or heavy colors. The Colonial

VICTORIAN
PERIOD

Arrangement by Mrs. Anne
Elizabeth Erhorn

FRENCH
PERIOD

Arrangement by Mrs. Dexter
M. Ferry, Jr.

*FLEMISH
PERIOD*

*Arrangement by Mrs.
Anne Elizabeth Erhorn*

*COLONIAL
PERIOD*

*Arrangement by Mrs. John
H. Squires, Jr.*

167

may be less formal, but is not necessarily so. The container can be of glass. The French, except for the Provincial, is by contrast somewhat more sophisticated.

The *Georgian* period is influenced by the great English cabinetmakers and silversmiths of the eighteenth century. Adam, Chippendale, Hepplewhite, and others have left their heritage in fine wood. Silver candelabra and epergnes were much used on the dining tables. Flowers were placed in formal vases of porcelain, silver, or crystal in the drawing rooms. Today we regard the Georgian arrangement as a dignified, rich, rather symmetrical handling of the finest type of flowers combined with an elegant restraint in the choice and use of accessories.

The *Victorian* period was the essence of the nineteenth century. Its great merit was the initiative of the people to break away from the affectation of pseudo-classicism. Like the padded contours of the horsehair sofas of that era, their flower arrangements were a full, rather stiff handling of old-fashioned flowers. Dark, rich colorings were used as well as pure white. A massed effect was considered desirable. Elaborately decorated, often ornate containers, such as the "flare"-shaped Victorian vase, also alabaster vases, porcelain urns, as well as containers of bronze were much used. Today, Victorian furnishings are being revived in a rather amusing way. Modern Victorian flower arrangements can echo that trend. It seems senseless to spend precious time and energy as well as flowers to try to copy something that can never really be attractive. The truly mid-Victorian flower arrangement had best be forgotten.

The twentieth century ushered in the *Modern* period. Here the French moderns—such as Cézanne, Renoir, Monet—paved the way.

Good modern flower arrangements are characterized by clear-cut plant forms and color. Bold masses of color, line, and form are constructed to blend or contrast with a modern setting. This is the streamlined style with a complete absence of confusing detail. Containers made of any of the modern materials, such as stainless steel, plastics, heavy modern crystal and glass, as well as pottery, are available and suitable.

Contemporary arrangements are not necessarily "modern" in the true sense of that term, although they can be. A contemporary flower arrangement is rather one which is suitable for any period type of house—that is, blended or "geared" to present-day living.

In summing up period arrangements it seems important to stress this fact: Whatever period your house may be, it is the most important setting for you and your family. Surely it is worthy of your greatest artistic efforts. Study its style and adapt the knowledge that you have gained from your study of flower arrangements. If you are too busy to have elaborate arrangements, plan simple basic designs which need not be changed every day. So often we hear people say: "Oh, that arrangement is just for my home; it would never do for a show!" Surely your home is more important than any flower show, and yet what slaves we are when preparing for competition. We are still young in this field of art expression. We need to learn a true sense of values and where and how best to express them.

Arrangement by Mrs. John Delafield

MODERN: Bold, strong silhouette, rectangular forms, few flowers, and dramatic foliage characterize most of the really "modern" arrangements. Materials used here are Chrysanthemums, Paulownia seed pods, and highly colored Croton leaves.

CHAPTER XV

Modern Arrangements

The term "modern arrangements" has been employed in a dual sense and hence has led to considerable confusion on the part of those interested in studying the art of arranging flowers.

By some writers and lecturers any arrangement done in the present-day manner—that is, untrammeled by the "rules" of any particular school or the design pattern of any particular "period"—is considered a modern arrangement. A better term to use here would be "contemporary arrangement."

Another and a more specific use of the term is when it is employed to designate arrangements which are "modern" in the same sense in which we speak of "modern" art. Here any exact definition is difficult—as it's easy to realize if you have ever listened to a dissertation on modern art! But in general there is the implication of a more definite and violent breaking away from the traditional—a striking out for new and often startlingly dramatic effects.

Contemporary Arrangements

Keeping the difference between these two definitions in mind, we may more intelligently discuss the general subject.

Contemporary arrangements are of the type which we have principally talked about all through this book, and so we need not go into great detail discussing them here. They are marked by freedom and informality, a discarding of the customary design patterns of both oriental and earlier occidental arrangements. In a word, our contemporary arrangers might be called the "do-as-you-please school"—and what you please may or may not be "modern" in the more limited application of the word.

In contemporary arrangements either mass or line may predominate (pages 123 and 170); or the two may be so combined that it is difficult to say whether the result would be classed as mass or line (page 287).

A distinct new tendency in contemporary arrangements is toward a three-dimensional design—one that can be looked *into* as well as at. An example of this type is shown on page 15. "Depth" is especially important in arrangements made for home decoration, as these are seldom viewed from one angle only—as show arrangements usually are. Even with show arrangements, however, depth is a factor that may well be kept in mind; judges are getting more and more depth conscious.

Depth is attained in two ways. First, by building the sides of the arrangement farther around toward the back, thus giving a broader surface of display when viewed from either side. Second, by so placing the materials—even important elements —that some of them will be set back in the mass instead of their all being more or less in one plane when viewed from the front. These methods of attaining greater depth are exemplified in the arrangements on pages 53 and 112.

Another characteristic of contemporary arrangements is the bold use of color contrasts. These can be made dramatic without one's going completely wild—a type of experimenting that is better left to those who wish to try really "modern" compositions. Arrangements in which many different colors are grouped together—a polychrome harmony—are often attractive but seldom really striking.

Still another characteristic of contemporary arrangements is the employment of unusual forms. Here the imagination of the arranger can be given free rein—subject, of course, to the controls exercised by adhering to the general principles of good composition and design.

"*Modern*" *Arrangements*

The "modern" arrangement, as already implied, is difficult to isolate other than to say in general that it possesses the characteristics we associate with "modern" art. Fortunately, the flower arranger, with the best (or should we say the worst?) intentions in the world cannot possibly go quite so haywire as the artist who uses canvas and paint. Even the cleverest manipulator of blossoms and foliage, for instance, would fail in the attempt to make a melted-cheese timepiece out of a Sunflower or a Tulip.

The characteristics you will find in most "modern" arrangements are bold, out-of-the-ordinary design; geometric forms, either in the design or the material, including containers, bases, and accessories; clean-cut, sharp silhouette; and color combinations that range far from the usual. Often plant material is trimmed at sharp angles; flower petals are reflexed or pulled out; vegetables may be cut to simulate flowers (very nifty rosebuds can be made from small beets, for instance); or other alterations or distortions are resorted to.

Arrangements in the extreme modern manner are often great attention-getters at flower shows; they seldom have a merited place in home decoration—except in surroundings that in themselves are so extreme that bizarre decorations, floral or otherwise, are in keeping.

To say all this is by no means to condemn utterly the extremely modern in flower arrangements. There is no question about their helping to lend interest to flower-show schedules and to pep up the arrangement sections of flower shows. Constructing them is excellent practice in design—and is worth while for that reason if for no other.

Can You Be Original?

From the foregoing it will be evident that *originality* is a prime requisite in the making of good modern arrangements. With practice almost anyone can master the mechanical details of how to put a flower arrangement together—but the sixty-four-dollar question still remains: "How can I make my arrangement original—give it that something that will make it stand out from run-of-the-mill compositions?"

As you begin to acquire skill in producing arrangements which are something more than just bouquets of pretty blossoms, your inclination at first—quite naturally—will be to copy, or at least imitate, good work you have seen at flower shows, in photographs, or in other people's homes. But if you desire to win a reputation as a good arranger, you will not be content to remain a copyist. And this brings us to the most difficult of all phases of flower arranging to attempt to explain, or to give instructions in: the knack of creating compositions that will have distinction *and* originality.

Let us be frank and admit at the outset that no amount of study and practice will assure success in this particular. In these pages we have frequently compared flower arranging to other arts, especially painting. Here again the comparison holds true. Of aspiring painters who fairly well master the techniques of painting, not one in a thousand succeeds in doing work that is both excellent technically and genuinely original. There remains a certain something that can never be acquired by practice nor imparted by instruction: *that is a gift with which the artist must be endowed by nature.*

But even with this admission made—and accepted—there is no reason why the student should not attempt to attain to some degree of originality in his work. Certainly he will get farther along the road by making a conscious, and conscientious, effort in this direction than if he merely trusts to luck and "inspiration."

What Constitutes Originality?

Almost any observer of a group of flower arrangements will realize that there are occasionally a few which "have something" that is not possessed by the others—quite aside from their technical perfection. Indeed, the arrangement which has this "something" may be far from perfect technically.

If, however, you should ask an admirer of the outstanding arrangement just why it appealed to him, you would probably have difficulty in getting a cogent answer. We have tried that experiment often, and the reply most frequently given is: "I can't say exactly, but it *does* something to you."

That, of course, is not of much help. But if you attempt to analyze such an arrangement, ninety-nine times out of a hundred you will find that it is extremely simple and clean-cut in design, and that (whatever may be its other faults) it possesses *unity* in a high degree. So with that much of a guide to start with, let us see what additional pointers of a practical nature we can unearth to assist us.

How Be Original? What can one do to attain originality in making a flower arrangement? Are there any "basic principles" that can be learned, such as those which apply to the technique of making a good arrangement?

The broad answer to the latter question is "no." But it is possible to give some suggestions that may prove helpful, even though true originality is not to be attained by any set of rules.

Plan. The starting point is the general plan or theme for the arrangement. In an earlier chapter we emphasized the desirability of having a clear mental picture of what the finished composition will be like before starting to put it together. This is doubly important if you wish to create something that will be out of the ordinary. It is a comparatively easy matter to take a given lot of cut-flower material and foliage (provided they harmonize satisfactorily as to colors) and work out, as one goes along, a creditable arrangement in the familiar crescent, curve, or radiating design. But an arrangement of real distinction is seldom so achieved. It starts with a definite *idea,* and has a longer germinating period.

The crux of the matter is where the idea is to come from; what will be its genesis. Here different arrangers work differently. One may get an inspiration from a unique container, and then hunt out unusual plant material to go with it. Another may proceed just the other way around. But always there is the searching for the idea that will make this particular arrangement different from the cooked-over-again constructions that bore judges at flower shows and leave connoisseurs who visit your home a bit embarrassed as to just what to say about your attempts at floral decoration.

DESIGN. With the general plan or idea of the arrangement decided upon, your next problem is to work out the design. Keeping in mind that your special interest at the moment is to put the emphasis on *originality,* discard the more or less standardized treatments that will occur to you. You will need to do some mental experimenting—to try one mind's-eye picture after another until you feel that you can say, "That's it; that's the idea I've been looking for." Some arrangers find it helpful at this point to make rough sketches of design-ideas that occur to them. Such a sketch, no matter how rough, is helpful because it must be definite: it tends to bring the mental picture into sharp focus.

MATERIAL. It is possible to make commonplace flowers and containers into a flower arrangement that has genuine originality but it is much easier to get an original effect if both plant material and container are unusual. But do not be misled into thinking that unusual materials will assure an original arrangement—they merely make a difficult task somewhat easier. They are helpful not only because they themselves contribute to the effect of originality, but also because they are likely to suggest *designs* that possess originality.

That is why so many arrangers who have a reputation for doing original work are always on the lookout for forms of

Arrangement by Mrs. Robert Kearfott

EMPHASIS ON FORM: In this modern arrangement the artist has employed extremes of plant form, as well as of color, to obtain a strikingly dramatic effect. A fine example of the skillful use of contrast *for emphasis.*

plant material not ordinarily used in arrangements. The beginner is likely to think only in terms of flowers, but often foliage or seed pods offer quite as much. Such material need not be exotic. The broad, velvety-gray leaves of a Mullein, the polished rich mahogany "hood" of a Skunk-cabbage, the brilliant-berried Jack-in-the-pulpit—such simple things as these challenge the imagination of the arranger, and may spark the idea that will result in a really original arrangement.

CONTAINERS. Another source for ideas that may lead to out-of-the-ordinary arrangements is to be found in unusual containers. Some of the most original—and most pleasing—arrangements in recent shows have been achieved with containers made by the exhibitor; such containers, for instance, as those made from weatherworn or water-worn roots of trees, as typified in the arrangements shown on pages 180 and 227. It is a fascinating hobby to hunt out material that lends itself to such use, and to shape and finish it to the desired form. Ordinarily the first step is to clean out all soil and loose tissue with a wire brush. Then with knife or sharp chisel do such reshaping as may be needed; an inexpensive set of wood-carving tools is handy for this purpose. Finally a watertight cylinder of suitable size is inserted in a hole made for the purpose, or secured to the back of the piece; any tinsmith, if provided with a rough sketch, can make one of these. The wood may be left natural, or stained or varnished, as you want.

Other prolific sources for unusual containers—as suggested in a previous chapter—are antique shops. Even the humblest junk shop is not to be sneezed at as a possibility.

ACCESSORIES. Not infrequently the arrangement scheme may start with an accessory. But here you are playing with fire. The accessory itself may be novel and interesting, but only if the arrangement is so designed as to tie in with it, in a subtle or dramatic manner, will the result be good. (See photograph on page 69.) Accessories, like containers, may be discovered in many places other than flower shops. Hunting them out is an amusing part of the game.

EMPHASIS. Finally—when you are attempting to do something original in the way of an arrangement—there is the matter of *emphasis*. Keep in mind that you cannot successfully make it a three-ring circus. If you try to stress originality in plant material, in container, and in accessories, all at one time, you are pretty certain to fall between three stools.

If your plant material is sufficiently original, trust to that, and to the design into which you work it, to carry your point. Let the container be suitable but not too prominent; accessories absent or quite subordinate. With a particularly effective container, the plant material should be such that it will not "steal the show." If accessories are sufficiently good to be the center of attraction (a situation that is very unusual though an example may be seen on page 81), then you will be wise to give them the limelight, and let the accompanying plant materials and container play up to them.

Apply rigorously all these checks—as to design, scale, balance, harmony, focus, rhythm, and unity—which have previously been discussed. You can keep within bounds on these general principles and still create an arrangement that will not be stilted and commonplace. Your objective must be to make an arrangement that will not merely possess originality but be, in addition, a really good arrangement.

DRY
ARRANGEMENTS

Compositions made with dry or dormant materials have the advantage of lasting for a long time and offer a field for intriguing experiment. They can be quite colorful too.

Arrangements by Mrs. Dunham C. Jones and Mrs. Erik A. Thomee

CHAPTER XVI

Arrangements of Dried Materials

BY ESTHER G. WHEELER

Don't too quickly assume that arrangements made with dried and dormant materials can be nothing more than a handful of milkweed stalks stuck in a bean pot to scatter their silken beauty about the room for two or three weeks, and then gather dust until they are finally consigned, in desperation, to the ashcan. Some of the most lovely—and the most dramatic too—of flower-show arrangements in recent years have appeared in the "dry-material" classes. And equally pleasing things can be done for the home.

Flower arrangements to augment other room decorations are now considered a must in our aesthetic existence. The material for them presents no great problem at a time when our gardens are producing and when the waysides and fields are teeming with wild growths of all kinds. Then we may gorge to our heart's content and fill our rooms with any number of live flower arrangements. This wealth of material, unfortunately, is not available to us the year around. When summer wanes and autumn arrives we must look elsewhere for a substitute.

War taught us conservation, so we may now practice it by substituting "everlasting" designs and arrangements of dried plant material for those oft-renewed live bouquets of summer; provided, of course, we had the foresight to have a supply on hand. To insure this wintertime stock, we should preserve the summertime products of the flower garden by the simple expedient of drying them. Suggestions on how to dry them are given later in this chapter.

Materials for Dried Arrangements

In providing materials for dried arrangements it is necessary to secure as great a variety as possible. Of course there will not be so wide a range as with fresh material, but with a little ingenuity one may accumulate a veritable treasure chest from which to draw many adaptable specimens for the composition of "everlastings" at a time when garden flowers have long ceased to bloom. While being far from inclusive, they are suggested as good types because of their interesting forms, good color, and excellent drying propensities.

For Color—to avoid monotonous effects—use these garden flowers: Acrolinium, daisy-like heads; crimson and golden crested Cockscomb; *Celosia spicata,* silvery rose; Gomphrena, brilliant magenta and orange clover heads; golden Ageratum, richest yellow; golden Yarrow, fragrant; Roses, red, heavily petaled varieties; *Salvia farinacea,* wedgewood blue; Sea-lavender, silvery lavender; Tansy, light yellow disks; Winged Everlasting, white; Zinnias, double-flowered varieties. These wild flowers also: Curly Dock, dark brown fruits; feathery Goldenrod; Queen Anne's Lace—pick when dry; Smooth Sumac, red; and Thistle, white.

For background use ornamental grasses, reeds, and grains: Bamboo, gray; miniature Cattails (dip heads in shellac to prevent opening); Cloud Grass, tufted; Natal Grass, reddish flowers; Fountain Grass; Pampas Grass; Job's Tears, dry flower panicles; Barley and Broom Corn, tan; Millet, dark brown; Oats and Rye, beige; Sorghum, tan to dark brown; Macaronia Wheat, beige; and Timothy, green.

Interesting Forms are found in many seed pods. They must be gathered before they open, else they lose their form. Some suggestions are: *Baptisia australis* and Blackberry Lily;

Arrangement by Mrs. John R. Fisher
Courtesy Colonial Williamsburg

   Dry material used in the Colonial manner, for an autumn bouquet.

such spear-type forms as Catalpa, *Carolina thermopsis,* Iris, and Rose-acacia; round forms, such as Monarda, Erigeron, Honesty, Globe-thistle, Poppy, Chinese Lanterns, and Peony. On the roadside we find Amsonia, Butterfly-weed, Honey Locust, Tulip Tree, Sumac, Milkweed, Climbing Milkweed (South Carolina), and Mullein. There are many varieties of unusual seed pods: Eucalyptus; the heart-shaped brown ones of the Baobab tree; tropical Allamanda; the curiously twisted ones of Sandalwood, filled with scarlet berries; the Lotus; and the Traveler's Tree, with its fuzzy electrifying turquoise-blue berries. The latter must be picked at least four weeks before they open.

FOR FILLER, use such leaves as: Artemisia, gray; Beech and Fern (press between newspaper sheets); Cardoon, coarsely cut; Horseradish, twisted forms; Leatherleaf Viburnum, rich green; Mullein (use as rosettes for accent); Palmetto leaves (trim before drying); and leaves of Canna, autumn Oak, and Southern Magnolia. To preserve indefinitely, place stems in one third glycerine and two thirds water.

DRAMATIC LINES in arrangements, to emphasize design, are readily obtained with dried bare branches. They may be the gnarled branches of Wisteria, Magnolia, Winged Euoynmous, Manzanita, weathered Cedar and Birch, as well as the brilliant colored berried branches of Barberry, Black Alder, and Bittersweet. Cones of Hemlock, Spruce, and Pine may be used to advantage; also fruits and vegetables. In this category are: Artichokes; Gourds, both *cucurbita* and *lagemaria,* which must be harvested after a slight frost, cut with long stems, and hung in a dry place; hot Peppers—Hungarian Wax, yellow and red, and Cayenne, red. In this class might come the ornamental Corns, such as Strawberry, Red Rice, and the Inca's Corn of Mexico.

Pointers on Drying and Using

During the productive spring and summer months our flower gardens can be made to do double duty. Besides supplying our freshly cut specimens currently, surpluses may be set aside and preserved for arrangements of dried materials during the winter. Plant material can be dried with a minimum amount of time and effort and with only a limited knowledge, and with little or no planning.

To dry flowers and preserve their natural color, they should be cut when they first come into bloom, or when just showing color. Foliage should be stripped to prevent continued growth, and they should be tied into bunches and left to hang upside down in a dark, dry place, so that the moisture may evaporate quickly.

Arrangement by Mrs. Innis Brown

Dry materials are well adapted to the type of modern
arrangement in which special emphasis is placed on form
and line. Here the circle motif, established with the
container, is repeated with the Magnolia leaves and again
with the branches.

When grouping dried material into appropriate designs, containers may be of brass, copper, pewter, or pottery. Gourds, logs, and Coconut sheaths may be utilized also. Woven mats and burlap with dried materials attached are used for decorative wall panels.

To secure dried material in an arrangement, use pinholders and florist's clay in a low container, covering with old moss or weathered stones. Fill a tall container with sand, top it with clay, and stick stems through the clay into the sand. To support tender stems, use stems of Willow, wire, or Bamboo.

The use of dried plant material for Christmas decorations is not only appropriate and practical but is becoming increasingly popular. The ephemeral aspect of cut flowers during that season, in contrast with the permanence and durability of dried materials, is an argument for using the latter.

Moreover, memory of Christmases elsewhere may be preserved by using: California Pepper berries and Yucca seed pods; Florida Coconut calyxes; Canadian Spruce and Hemlock cones; or the Desert-Holly of Arizona, et cetera, all of which have highly decorative value.

Fresh plant material, if available, or the ever-increasingly hard-to-get evergreens combine well with them, permitting a wide variation of creations such as a rich brown wreath of cones and seed pods of the Camphor tree with bold accents of magenta-crested Cockscomb and bunches of golden Ageratum. Here Bayberries, Southern Magnolia seed pods, Rose hips, or red berries of the English Yew or Black Alder, may be substituted. A Victorian rose wreath of Coconut calyxes painted white with gold centers and sprinkled with tinsel, all fastened on a ten-inch ring of wire or an eighteenth-century bell pull, made up in the Della Robbia manner, has proven popular. For the latter use chicken wire, $3\frac{1}{2}''$ by $36''$, backed with green cloth as the base of the bell pull. Fill in with shellacked cones, Lotus pods, dried fruits and nuts, and other dried material. Small bells or shellacked groupings of Cranberries, Lady Apples, or Limes may be substituted.

The pleasure and satisfaction to be derived from fashioning decorations with the materials one has collected and preserved

Arrangement by Mrs. Frank C. Boes

Seeds and seed pods. Sorghum, withered foliage and Grasses in a design that goes well with the Oriental figure used as an accessory.

more than compensates for the effort expended in collecting them. Especially so when it permits "casual" decorations, free from yardsticks and rule-of-thumb manipulation. They are not only appropriate and practical, but they are economical— particularly for Christmas, when there are so many extra calls on the budget.

Arrangement by Mrs. Jesse Thomas Fort

Here the plant material—Magnolia flowers, buds, and foliage—is very nicely arranged, but the container is just a trifle small. A long base under the container—such as might have been used in a flower show—would have improved the balance.

CHAPTER XVII

Miniature Arrangements

BY CLAIRE STICKLES

A miniature arrangement might be called the Lilliputian of the flower show. During the past few years the miniature has grown in popularity with the exhibitors as well as the general public. Those who come to the flower shows marvel at the cleverness of the arrangements, and the miniature exhibit usually is a very popular spot in the show. This popularity has resulted in a greatly increased use of miniatures for home decoration.

The term "miniature" is often misunderstood by exhibitors. A miniature differs from a "small" arrangement. I have seen so-called miniatures in flower shows that really were small arrangements. Some authorities consider a miniature should not be more than three inches over all, while others claim that six inches is a better size. A six-inch arrangement does give more opportunity to make a pleasing design and greater freedom of expression. A tiny three-inch arrangement, when well done, is a work of art, but most of us would have to use a magnifying glass to see its beauty.

Whether arrangers are intrigued by the use of small containers and small-plant material, or whether they would rather work on a small-scale arrangement is the question. Nevertheless, the miniature definitely has its place and should be included in all flower shows.

A miniature arrangement may develop from an idea, an interesting container, or a flower-show schedule, but you must always keep in mind the space where the arrangement is to be placed. The first important step is the selection of a suitable container. A class may designate the type of an arrangement to be made and the container should be in keeping with that idea.

Collecting miniature containers and accessories can be made a very fascinating hobby. There are so many miniature vases, bottles, bowls, and other articles that find their way into a flower show that are charming and sometimes amusing. One has but to rummage around a child's room to find some dainty little toy or tea set, with its sugar bowl, creamer, and teapot. Any one of them would make an interesting container for a miniature.

One may find in a department store a vast assortment of tiny perfume vials; or perhaps an old lipstick tube that's been lying around the house would serve for a cylinder container. Tiny seashells, such as conch, snail, or the flat little mussel shells are often winners in a flower show. A silver thimble or a walnut is easy to use as a container. From Mexico and other foreign lands come colorful bits of pottery, glass, china, and metal in many shades and shapes. One can make a few containers for their collection from soap and potter's clay. Small low dishes or bowls are easily made by cutting a piece of soap two inches long, one inch deep, and one inch wide. Hollow out the center deep enough to hold water. A thin layer of melted para-wax on the inside will seal the soap so that the container will hold water. The little dish will have the appearance of alabaster.

Potter's clay can be modeled easily into small bowls or flat containers and baked in a very hot oven until the clay is set. Paint the container with oil paints, then shellac for a glaze and para-wax the inside. These little containers are fascinating and with care will last a long time. Another idea is the use of a bantam eggshell. Pierce the shell on one end with a needle and break the shell on the other end a little smaller than a dime, then blow the egg out of the shell. Seal the needlepoint hole with a bit of waterproof glue and paint the container any color you wish to use. A small base may be made of clay. In order

At any flower show the class for miniatures is sure to be well filled. This "window" method of staging them—used at the International Flower Show in New York—not only saves space, but gets the arrangements up to eye level.

for the shell to set on the base, press the shell into the damp clay, to get the impression, and when the clay is baked it will fit the end of the egg. The shell is then filled with sand to give it weight and also to hold the plant material.

Accessories should be selected as carefully as containers. Tiny little figures can be carved out of the soap and used as accessories. A penknife and an orange stick are about all the tools needed for the carving and modeling.

Small bases add a finishing touch to an arrangement. They may be "discovered" in much the same way as the containers. A discarded cold-cream top or pocket mirror will serve. I have seen poker chips in the various colors used as bases.

One could go on endlessly with suggestions of what to use for miniature arrangements. Fabrics also add a charm to the

191

flower picture and they, too, must be in harmony both in color and texture.

There are a few tools needed in making a miniature arrangement. Tweezers with a small point and a very small pair of embroidery scissors are most important, unless one wishes to lose one's mind trying to handle the very small plant material with fingers. No matter how deft one's hands may be, fingers do get in the way!

Miniature arrangements are flower compositions on a small scale and the principles which govern a larger arrangement apply in building a miniature composition. The arrangement must have design, balance, and rhythm. Above all, avoid giving your miniature the appearance of being overcrowded. Each tiny flower and bit of foliage should show its own beauty.

The selection of the plant material depends to a great extent on the type of container to be used. A slender container with a small neck would need slender foliage, such as blades of grass or foliage of the Grape-hyacinth, and would be interesting with the flowers of the dainty Sweet Alyssum. In a bowl-like container, naturally the flowers should be more on the buxom side. A design is sometimes suggested by a curve or an angle of a stem or the formation of a flower. On that basis, a design should begin to formulate in your mind. Select a container that would be suitable for the design you have planned.

Textures play an important part in an arrangement. Coarse flowers need a coarse container, such as pottery or metal, while the dainty flower material will be more pleasing arranged in glass or silver. Flowers and foliage are most important in a miniature arrangement as to size and scale.

As already suggested, tiny blades of grass or the foliage of the Grape-hyacinth are good for height. The curly ends of the Wisteria or the Wild Onion give distinction to the arrangement. White Clover foliage would be good for the base of the arrangement. One has only to walk along the roadside to find interesting flower material. Yellow Buttercups, wild Dill, fall Asters, Blue-eyed-grass, Bluets, and Fringed Orchis are just a few one might find in the wild. In the meadow there are many

Arrangement by Mrs. Wendell Kilmer

Miniature in close up. Except for the dime in the corner that gives it scale it might be taken for a full-size arrangement. The container is a trifle tall for height of plant material—as will be seen by blotting out pyramidal base with a fingertip.

colored grasses with their graceful seed heads. Forget-me-nots, Gypsophila, Sweet Alyssum, Ageratum, and Lily-of-the-valley are all suitable plant material. There are very few Roses (aside from the "baby" Roses such as Oakington, Ruby, and *Rosa roulleti*) that can be used in miniatures because of their size, but the half-open buds of small-flowered Ramblers and Hybrid Teas may serve.

For miniatures I have used small pieces of Scotch Broom bent to provide a graceful line, and for accent the center of a Poinsettia after the bracts had dropped off. Small flowerets of Lilac or Buddleia are in proper scale for a miniature arrangement. Acacia, with its bright yellow spray and gray-green foliage, combined with the tiny blossoms of a red Begonia, would be a pleasing combination.

It is not always necessary to consider a miniature from a flower-show standpoint. Much pleasure can be given to a "Shut-in" by making a small dish garden of miniature material. Small metal pans may be made of plumbers' lead. They are sturdy and strong and will not rust. A few small pebbles in the bottom of the pan for drainage, and soil suitable for the needs of the plants, and you are ready to make a little dish garden.

A few vines and seedlings from the woods, such as tiny Pines or Hemlocks and Partridge berries, will go well together. This little garden will gladden the heart. Near the edge of a brook one may find the tiniest type of creeping plant material and baby Ferns. The Fern will in time outgrow the scale of the miniature dish garden and will have to be replaced. To make the composition more naturalistic, use a few colored or odd-shaped stones in it. Tiny little animal accessories, such as deer, might be added, as the woodland is their natural habitat.

One of the best ways to interest children in the love of flowers and plant material is to get them to help collect wild flowers and plants. Many garden clubs are including children's exhibits in their flower shows, and the keen interest that the children display in their efforts is very gratifying. With their small hands they seem more adept at managing the small material than do most grownups. Children are born imitators, and, if we wish them to grow up with an interest in how to use flowers as an important element in home decoration, now is the time to start them making small and miniature arrangements.

Arrangement by Mrs. Esther Wheeler

A miniature in which the scaling is just about perfect. The Trumpet Daffodil gives an idea of its actual size.

Arrangement by Mrs. Robert C. Bourne

The wall arrangement—much less frequently used than it might be—saves table space, provides maximum display for flowers.

CHAPTER XVIII

Table and Wall Arrangements

No meal is quite complete without a decoration of plant material to grace the board. Time is well spent by the homemaker who realizes this fact and makes the most of it to improve the appearance of her table and lift the spirits of those who sit around it.

General Pointers

1. The first and most important thing to remember about table decorations is that they must be low enough not to interfere with the diners' view of one another. Tall bouquets are not conducive to general table conversation.

2. Another point which will bear stressing is that a table arrangement should be attractive at every angle from which it may be seen. The only exception to this (and to the matter of height as well) is the floral decoration for a buffet table, placed against the wall. In this case a three-sided arrangement, tall or low as desired, is in perfect order.

It is not necessary to fill a vase with a symmetrical mass of flowers in order to make it beautiful from every side. When a line composition is used, such as a branch of flowering fruit tree with flowers such as Crocuses or Muscari near the base, place a group of the low-growing blooms at each side of the flowering spray, thus making it attractive also when viewed from the two ends of the table.

Sometimes it is desirable to have an arrangement that can be observed from any angle. Here are views, from opposite sides, of an "all-around" composition. (See opposite page.)

In other low table groupings—especially long, narrow ones —this method can be used. Simply make two similar one-sided arrangements, placing them back to back in the container, the high, medium, and low points of each coinciding with the other. This applies also to groups of fruits and vegetables as well as to flowers or foliage; and to combinations of any two or all four of these.

When a very shallow dish is used and flowers are placed just above the water level so that they seem to float on the surface, it is a simple matter to make the picture attractive from every viewpoint.

3. In planning an arrangement for a table, the shape of the board is first taken into consideration. A round table will set

off a round, square, plumply oval, or oblong composition. The longer the table, the longer the container and arrangement can be. On a very long table, two arrangements are often used and these may be tied together with accessories such as glass or silver birds or other figurines, candelabra, et cetera. A long candleholder with a number of candles burning may occupy the center of a long table with an arrangement at each end of it.

4. Arrangements for tables should be planned in relation to the total effect, a composition *of which they are only a part.* The colors, textures, and atmosphere of table covering, dishes, and other accessories—even of the type of food to be served—are guides to the floral decorations. These may blend or contrast in color but must be in the spirit of the whole. Garden flowers in pottery, wood, pewter, or copper containers will suit a very informal table setting. Fine or exotic flowers in appropriate containers are used for formal or daintily "pretty" table settings. A table featuring French dishes, for instance,

could appropriately be decorated with Bulbous Iris and Lilacs. A Mexican breakfast or lunch could best be set off with such colorful garden flowers as Zinnias and Marigolds.

Breakfast Tables

Though this is apt to be a hurried meal snatched in the breakfast nook or from the kitchen "bar" or counter, it can still be made more appetizing if there are fresh flowers on the board.

For every day, a pitcher of Nasturtiums or a jug of small annuals in bright colors is cheery in summer. Daffodils and other spring-flowering bulbs lend beauty in spring, and there are always hardy Chrysanthemums in autumn. For winter, use a pot of blooming African-violets or *Begonia semperflorens* in a pottery container.

On Sundays and holidays, when there is leisure to enjoy breakfast talk, make the day "special" with a more carefully arranged table bouquet as well as with more appetizing food. For breakfast parties, so popular nowadays, you can really let yourself go by doing a lovely table arrangement in the spirit of the occasion. Your guests will enjoy it quite as much as they do the food.

Luncheons

For weekday lunch, the breakfast bouquet may serve very well if you are rushed and overworked. But a better idea is to have another simple, unpretentious dish of flowers which can be substituted at this meal to give variety.

Since fruit is often a luncheon dessert, a well-arranged dish or tray of fruits may be used instead of flowers. A tray of Grapes with leaves and tendrils (harden these first in deep water for several hours) is beautiful and makes good eating. A generous bowl of Cherries or berries decorated with foliage is another thought, or a mixed group with large dark shapes placed low to give stability and with bits of foliage for height and horizontal lines.

Table by Mrs. John H. Squires, Jr.

Table settings give wide scope for the arranger to use originality. In these two examples the usual annoying hedge effect of a large centerpiece has been avoided by placing decorations at the ends.

Table by Mrs. J. C. Stark

For a formal luncheon the arrangement is more elaborate but less so than for a formal dinner. An attractive centerpiece can be made by grouping corsages or boutonnieres which are distributed to the guests at the close of the meal. The table then is not spotted over with small bouquets at each place. In general, tables look most inviting when they appear uncrowded and uncluttered. A bowl of short-stemmed Roses or Carnations can be used as a table center and one, two, or three distributed to each guest as a boutonniere when the luncheon is over.

For bridge luncheons very small, *low* vases, dishes, or other containers, uniform if possible, can be filled with colorful mixed flowers or with small short-stemmed nosegays of a single variety. One such bouquet is placed on each bridge table. For a large party such things as punch glasses, cocktail-sauce glasses, or low cocktail glasses can be pressed into service to hold the miniature arrangements. For a "one-table" evening with close friends, a still simple but larger arrangement, such as that shown on page 217, forms an attractive focus for the table itself. When the work of the evening begins, of course, the arrangement is removed and the playing surface left uncluttered except for cards and score pad.

Dinner

It is well for the hostess to keep on her closet shelves an adequate supply of containers which suit her dinner table when it is large or small, and suitable in material and design for formal and informal occasions, and for whatever table services may be used.

A delicate glass, silver, or porcelain dish is not appropriate with the pottery "rumpus" dishes, though perfect with the best china. For casual get-togethers an Oriental pottery dish or containers of wood, pewter, or copper are good.

When "floating" arrangements are used on the dinner table, select such flowers as Camellias, Gardenias, Moonflowers, full-blown Roses, Tuberous Begonias, or Waterlilies. Firmly fasten a pinpoint holder to the bottom of the dish with floral clay

Arrangement by Mrs. Fred W. Boschen, Jr., and Mrs. Harvey Traband, Jr.

Floral decorations for tables set for a few persons are frequently better placed at one side of the table instead of in the center.

before any water is used. Then add water to the dish and fasten short-stemmed flowers firmly in the tines of the holder so that each flower head is *just above* the water level; if the petals get waterlogged, they soon decay. Tendrils and vines are often effective in floating arrangements. Passionflowers, Moonflowers, or Cup-and-saucer Vine (*Cobaea scandens*) are especially good with their own foliage and decorative vine tips. Camellias, Gardenias, and Waterlilies also look well with their own leaves, or other broad-leaved evergreens can be substituted.

When buying florists' flowers for the dinner table, do not waste money on long stems. Select cheaper, short-stemmed but fresh Roses or other flowers, and use a low bowl or dish. Half-a-dozen white Anemone-flowered Chrysanthemums can be used to make a beautiful composition. Place a graceful, horizontally branching spray of coniferous or broad-leafed evergreen in a long Oriental dish, fastening it firmly in a pinpoint holder. Arrange a few short-stemmed Chrysanthemums on each side of the branch at its base, full-blown flowers just above the water line, buds higher. Let a white quartz rock or two peep out of the water at the other end of the dish. Fresh flowers can be substituted as needed. The evergreen branch will stay fresh for several weeks.

If a very formal table is desired, and you wish to use one or two symmetrical mass arrangements in urns or other classic containers, select *low* vases, and give the compositions greater breadth than height. Use Montbretias, Sweet Peas, Freesias, or other airy flowers for the necessary height and breadth rather than the heavy spikes of Snapdragon, Stocks, or Gladiolus. Larger blooms can be utilized for the focal centers.

For line or semi-line arrangements, use two similar groupings placed back to back as already described.

Buffet Tables

Here you can really let yourself go, since no one is to sit at the table. If food and service are to be placed all around the table, the arrangement goes in the center. For a long table, two groupings may be used. For a table against a wall, place the decoration all the way back, just clearing the wall.

For a buffet, you can use any material which suits your fancy, your table service, and the spirit of the party.

At a hunt breakfast, red Gladiolus, Dahlias, or Geraniums give a riot of the right color. If an Italian note is to be struck for a spaghetti supper, use an Italian pottery container with flowers in strong rich reds and golds. An Onion *soupe feste* could be graced with a centerpiece decoration of culinary herbs arranged in a broad French earthenware baking dish.

The formal buffet table can be decorated with a symmetrical mass arrangement in an elaborate porcelain urn or other handsome vase. Here you can use all the flowers in the list: Stocks and Snapdragons for height; Lilies, Roses, Tulips, and Carnations for focal interest; Freesias for airy side lines and sweet scent; Pansies, Anemones, and Gerberas for variety. Or a modern composition may be preferred, symmetrical or asymmetrical as the case may be, featuring a few very large showy flowers and striking accessory foliage.

Table Decorations for Restaurants, Church Suppers, et cetera

A very bad tradition has grown up about decorating tables in public dining rooms. The almost invariable custom is to stick a few blossoms in a tall, flaring glass vase and plump it in the middle of the table. A small, low, attractive bouquet is not any harder to arrange, and is really enjoyed by the diners.

At a small hotel in New England some years ago I came to the table three times a day to find a glistening finger bowl with a few rambler Roses smiling at me. I have never forgotten it. This sort of thing could and should be done more frequently. For the tavern type of dining room, individual bean pots of garden flowers in bright colors; for the damask-covered table, a low glass dish with a few short-stemmed flowers.

Tables for Special Occasions

We no longer use red, white, and blue paper decorations on Washington's Birthday and Fourth of July, but we can have a suggestion of patriotism in the flowers, though the color combination should not be too glaring. A deep blue container with red and white flowers is better than using blooms of all three colors, since they do not combine naturally.

At Christmas, a real arrangement, adhering to the principles set forth in previous chapters, can be made of appropriate material. A large semi-permanent composition for the buffet is a good thought for either Christmas or Thanksgiving. It can be larger and more ornate than is possible on the table, and it need not be disturbed.

Of course fruit and vegetables are traditional for Thanksgiving, though rich-toned autumn flowers with red Oak leaves are equally good and can be given more distinction if well arranged.

Fruits and Vegetables

In arranging fruits and vegetables for the table, your chief problems are in the artistic use of forms and colors. The large, graceful shapes of Eggplants, Pineapples, Pumpkins, et cetera, form the heavy base material. Avocados, Pears, Apples, and Oranges come next, and finally the dainty small Lady Apples, Nuts, Kumquats, and Grapes. If Bananas are to be used, work a small hand of them into your design. Don't stick them in here and there at unknown angles like the rocks in a beginner's rock garden.

Let there be rhythm in the design. This may be suggested by the form of a central item of focal importance, such as a Pineapple; or by the shape of the dish or tray. Group the colors as you do in an arrangement of flowers. Never spot them about, like a pattern in calico. The rich green of the Avocado sets off the glossy purple of an Eggplant, and these are spotlighted by several Tangerines or a handful of Kumquats. The color though not the texture of the Eggplant is repeated in a bunch of rich purple Grapes.

Use broad-leaved evergreen foliage or sprigs of Ivy to tie the shapes together and to give a little height and some interesting side lines. Or a Pineapple top or two may give all the height needed. When possible, get Apples or other fruit with a bit of twig and a leaf attached. These can always be used to good advantage. Select Pears and Apples with at least one rosy cheek. Wash and carefully polish each piece before placing it in the composition.

Many of the most distinguished arrangements of fruit and vegetables shown in competition today are combined with flowers. The flower colors and textures are selected to blend with those of the other material, and they are worked into the design to look as though they grew there by some strange miracle. (See illustration on page 141.)

Wall Arrangements

Akin in some respects to table arrangements are those for walls; like the former, they are usually given too little special

Mrs. Harold L. Brooks. Courtesy New York Times

For most formal mantels the use of twin arrangements, in symmetrical balance, is the most satisfactory treatment.

thought and consideration, but when they are exceptionally well done they can be strikingly impressive. Though less popular today perhaps than some years ago, wall arrangements offer the arranger an excellent field in which to specialize. They fit especially well on the wall of a sun porch, open veranda, or cabana; and can be used to good advantage where space is at a premium, as in a breakfast nook, powder room, or dressing room.

For wall or hanging containers, by all means go to an Oriental shop, for it is there that you will find the best selection, both in shapes and materials. Choose a hanging boat dish for the bay window or the veranda and some crackle pottery ware wall vases for other purposes. You may also find containers of bamboo or basketry.

For the boat containers, the conventional arrangement is one which will suggest a sail. It is not necessary to go into the symbolism of Japanese boat arrangement, but a triangular grouping with the rhythm of wind in it is effective and can be adapted to Western arrangement fashions. Gracefully curving vines can often be incorporated in such a composition.

Vines, of course, suggest themselves as material for wall vases. Each spray should be selected with care and a rhythmic design worked out. Flowers can be used near the center just above the top of the vase for focal interest.

Fan-shaped bouquets also look well in wall vases. They can be worked out with such flowers as Gladiolus, Snapdragons, *Salvia farinacea,* Larkspur, or Delphiniums. Other flowers can be used with these to give weight and interest in the center.

Wild flowers from the meadows, like Daisies and Goldenrod, are good in wall vases for cabanas, cabins, and the like. Or sprays of evergreen can be used together with a few colorful blooms.

Wall and hanging vases are a nice hobby, especially if you have spots which particularly fit them. Make a collection of containers and experiment with the many possibilities for floral decoration which they offer. In this connection it will be helpful if you can come by some books on Japanese flower arrangement with illustrations of wall and hanging compositions. Do not slavishly copy what you see, but let it suggest to you original groupings which you can create from the material readily available.

CHAPTER XIX

For Special Occasions

Though the custom of using seasonal floral decorations indoors is so old that it predates history, people still want new ideas for holiday flowers. It seems that every possible word and thought on the subject must already have been expressed, yet new ones constantly crop up.

In planning floral displays for special occasions two main objectives should be kept in mind:

First. Good taste. In order to be timely, the arranger cannot sacrifice her sense of color harmony, good design, or dignity. Where accessories are to be used, appropriate to the occasion, try to make them an integral part of the whole, not too conspicuous or inharmonious. As an example, she can use fresh flowers rather than paper hatchets and candy cherries to suggest Washington's Birthday. For instance, a container made from a length of Cherry wood with the bark left on could be filled with red Carnations and green foliage.

Second. Originality. Tradition is important in holiday decoration, arrangements for anniversaries, et cetera; but the work of the arranger who can think of new, striking ways to use traditional material is always appreciated by those who discriminate between mediocrity and perfection.

Let us then first consider the chief holidays of the year, begining with:

Thanksgiving

This is the time for fruit, fruit and vegetable, or fruit, flower, and vegetable arrangements, representing the harvest of plenty.

Lady Apples, red Crabapples, Citrus fruits, especially Limes, if they are to be had, Grapes of all colors and sizes, the great orange-red Oriental Persimmons, red and gold and green Pears, Pineapples and Avocados are excellent fruit material.

Vegetables to use with the fruit, or alone, include small Pumpkins, red Cabbage, colorful Peppers, and Eggplants.

To these may be added decorative Gourds in all their rich variety of form and color, and Navajo and Strawberry dried Corn, husks and all. These are beautfully tinted in rich cream, wheat, and rosy pastels. By dampening the husks, they can be bent back from the corn and set in any desired lines or curves in which they remain when dried.

A tray of fruits and vegetables, set off by a sheaf of ripe wheat, is in the spirit of the occasion.

Use Laurel, Rhododendron, or coniferous evergreen foliage as a base or to provide a foil for colorful forms where needed. Red Oak leaves are good also. When Pine is used, cones may be added to the grouping.

When a fruit or vegetable arrangement rests on a board, a tray, or in a basket, the problem is comparatively easy, though care should be taken to follow a clear, uncrowded design. Do not just pile up materials haphazardly.

When fruits and flowers are combined in a vase, however, in a formal composition, the artist must resort to hidden wires to hold the fruit in place. As a rule, the flowers—rich Mums or tall Snapdragons, perhaps—give height, while the fruits are used for focal interest. Successful combinations of fruit and flowers are often made on trays, or in low dishes. For the table, make two similar low arrangements in harvest colors and place them back to back, so that there will be floral interest from whatever angle they are viewed. Complete the composition

Arrangement by Mrs. Anne Elizabeth Erhorn

Brimming abundance of the autumnal season is well conveyed in this colorful arrangement for a harvest festival. (Exotic material, which is allowable in a spring flower-show composition, would, in a home decoration, be replaced by local products.)

with skillfully placed fruits in harmonious colors. These are banked around the base of the arrangement and extend beyond it to the end of a long, narrow tray or dish.

Arrangement by Mrs. Horace Paul Dormon
Courtesy Pennsylvania Horticultural Society

Christmas centerpiece, in a shallow tray, of Pine, Juniper, Holly, Bayberry, and "Wooden Roses."

Christmas

The trend in Christmas decoration is toward new fields—or in some cases a return to very old ones.

The crèche has again appeared on many a holiday mantel after years of semi-oblivion as a decoration. Flanked by candles and nestled in evergreen boughs, the crèche makes a beautiful and dignified Christmas motif. A modern ceramic, crystal, or carved-wood Madonna is frequently used as a central point of interest, together with greens, silvered branches, and candles.

Rich formal wreaths patterned after Della Robbia and constructed of shellacked fruits, nuts, and cones have become popular for tables and indoor hanging.

Christmas balls heaped on frost-sprinkled evergreen boughs glisten on the holiday board.

Table decorations of fresh red or white flowers, combined with a broad-leaf evergreen and tall candles, have taken the place of the fruit or floral "centerpieces." Combinations of blue and white, blue and silver, and red and gold are often substituted for the traditional red and green.

Special table covers of good design, featuring angels, cherubs, stars, et cetera, are very definitely a part of modern Christmas decoration.

For the fruit enthusiast there are always Pomegranates and Limes in the stores at Christmas. Heap them in a crystal dish and deck with sprigs of Laurel to simulate natural foliage.

Valentine's Day

This is the sentimental holiday—the time for red Roses, white Camellias, scented Violets, and red and white Carnations.

Place the last-named combination in a golden quiver and let the Carnation heads fall over the string of a golden bow for a really traditional table arrangement. Or pack a heart-shaped dish closely with Carnation heads or Violets.

Washington's Birthday, Fourth of July, et cetera

Patriotic holidays in America put a real strain on the flower arranger. Red, white, and blue cannot be combined to make a harmony, analogous or complementary. Brave souls continue to try to make successful patriotic arrangements, but these seldom come off.

Unless you are one of those inspired individuals who can do the impossible, and do it well, why not compromise? Use only those colors which your arrangement can carry—red and white, or blue and white, rather than red, white, and blue. Sometimes the smallest touch of the third color can be used in a container or near by, as in an accessory. If you feel you must have all three colors, try a shield-shaped low container and pack in flower heads to represent the United States emblem or use an oblong dish and make a flag of closely set flower heads.

Easter

Floral decorations for this holiday are easy to make because it is the time of Lilies, and Lilies just about arrange themselves. Only a few are needed, whether you select Callas or Easter Lilies. Calla foliage, too, is chaste and inspiring with the tall, pointed, curled tips, and the graceful open leaves sometimes spotted with silver.

Spring flowers can be used if preferred—all the pageant of spring-flowering bulbs, Lilac, and blossoming shrubs. Easter is no problem even to the least accomplished arranger.

Other Occasions

Table decorations for the *young girl,* either on her birthday, her graduation, or other celebration, can feature Sweetheart Roses, Myosotis, Blue Lace-flower, Lilies-of-the-valley, and other daintily colored blossoms. A shoulder bouquet for each guest can be worked into the central arrangement as a border and distributed at the end of the meal.

White flowers fit the *bride,* and what they are to be is governed by the season and the family budget. Starting with Orchids, Roses, and Lilies-of-the-valley, the gamut runs through all white florists' flowers down to the humble but beautiful Sweet Pea, which can be massed to give lovely effects, especially if a few larger flowers are used for interest.

For the bride's table a round open dish of Roses and Lilies-of-the-valley may spill out on the table as a shower bouquet, each white ribbon ending in a fresh nosegay.

For informal weddings—according to the season—the following garden flowers can be used:

APRIL	—*White Narcissus*
MAY	—*White Tulips*
	—*Lily-of-the-valley*
	—*White Peonies*

Arrangement by Mrs. Eleanor Towne Carey, Jr.

For birthdays, anniversaries, homecomings, special guests, the simplest of arrangements, strategically placed, supply a spirit of welcome or good cheer that can be expressed in no other way.

Arrangement by Mrs. Arthur N. Peck

215

Arrangement by Mrs. C. Colton Tuttle

For Easter, an unusually good design with not unusual
flowers, foliage, container, and base.

Arrangement by Mrs. H. T. Langworthy

A touch of cheerful welcome can be added for any occasion with a simple arrangement—for example, a bridge game. (Such arrangements, of course, can be removed later if in the way.)

Arrangement by Mrs. George A. Lofland

Flowers for a sick friend are infinitely more expressive
if made up into an arrangement than if delivered loose
in a box. Here's a suggestion for one that can readily be
transported.

JUNE	—White Roses
	—Ismenes
	—White Japanese Iris
JULY	—White garden Lilies
	—White Gladiolus
AUGUST	—White garden Lilies
	—White Dahlias
	—White Snapdragons

In this arrangement for a dinner table, tiny bouquet favors for the ladies form a part of the composition. The arrangement is sufficiently open not to obstruct view across table or impede conversation.

SEPTEMBER—*White Hardy Chrysanthemums*
—*White Roses*
—*White China Asters*

OCTOBER —*White Chrysanthemums*

For the Golden Wedding, nothing surpasses yellow Roses, and they must, of course, be in a golden container—a gold epergne can be used; or an ornate classic porcelain urn, heavily decorated with gold leaf; or crystal encrusted with gold.

When decorating for a Stag Party or an essentially masculine affair like a Hunt Breakfast, it is well to bear in mind that most men like red and other strong, rich colors.

Use Dahlias, red and gold Snapdragons and Chrysanthemums. Red or orange Lilies, deep-toned Gladiolus, Bearded Iris—all these suit the occasion. The more daring the arrangement, the more it will appeal to the average male. Not for him the restrained subtleties of the advanced student in arrangement. Of course there are plenty of exceptions to prove the rule. But even the man interested in floral arrangement is apt to prefer a blaze of luscious colors in a composition ample and unrestrained.

For an outdoor barbecue, fill a copper pot with Dahlias or red and orange Marigolds. Or arrange Gladiolus in a tall earthenware or metal pitcher, using Canna foliage to enhance the rich blooms.

Church Decoration

Church decoration presents a peculiar problem to the arranger. There are ecclesiastical rules to be observed as well as the principles of arrangement. The subject cannot be adequately covered, but here are a few suggestions which may help the beginner.

1. The forms used should be bold and distinct, not feathery and confused. Each composition will be viewed from a distance and in subdued light.

2. Flowers in the church are subservient, not dominant. Their purpose is to lead the eye to the sacred objects which they enhance. Thus flowers near the altar cross are placed on each side, lower than the cross itself—and possibly behind it. Blooms or stems should never extend above or in front of it.

3. Flower decorations in the church are never placed where they will impede the service—at the altar rail, for instance.

Those who wish to inform themselves fully on this specialized subject can consult Katharine M. McClinton's volume, *Flower Arrangement in the Church.*

Arrangement by Mrs. John T. Scheepers

Church arrangements are quite likely to prove insignificant unless they are carefully planned in relation to their surroundings, background, and the fact that they will be viewed from a considerable distance.

Arrangement by Mrs. Reginald Wilson

A made-up base of Sphagnum or peat moss, to accommodate plants with roots, may be used in combination with a container to hold cut-flower material.

CHAPTER XX

Living-Plant Arrangements

The use of living plants in making arrangements is a practice which can often be employed to advantage. Compositions made with living plants alone, arranged for a more or less permanent effect, of course come under the category of indoor gardening rather than that of flower arrangement. What we are discussing here is the employment of growing plants, either by themselves or in combination with cut blooms, in the creation of floral designs of a temporary nature. Such temporary arrangements, made of living plants growing on their own roots, have much to recommend them. One carefully made composition of this type can be counted on to remain alive and in good condition for from one to three weeks.

Living-plant arrangements are really just a modern improvement on the Fern dish and the "Japanese garden." Instead of depending for decorative effect on a mass of green fronds in a silver basket or a group of miniature figures, bridges, and pagodas spotted among florists' plants, the arranger today selects plants just as she would choose blooms and foliage for a cut-flower composition. She combines these in accordance with the general principles of good composition and produces a group of living plants or a combination of plants and cut flowers which has design, focal interest, good balance, and unity.

Mechanics

Plants growing on their own roots must have endurable living conditions if they are to survive. In order to make your living-plant arrangements last as long as possible, the following points cannot be too greatly stressed.

1. SUITABLE CONTAINERS. Low dishes are usually most satisfactory but they must be deep enough to hold roots, soil, and drainage material. Tall, slender groupings may be placed in deeper pottery vases, pots, or bowls.

2. SANITATION. Plants cannot live in dry or soggy undrained soil. First of all place a layer of pebbles, crocking, or large cinders in the bottom of the container. Cover this with potting soil suitable to the plant material, mixing with it bits of charcoal to help keep the soil "sweet." After the composition is completed, be careful not to *overwater*, unless bog plants are used, and even then caution is necessary. For average garden or florists' plants, water only enough to keep the surface soil moderately damp.

3. COMPATIBILITY OF MATERIAL. Do not be too reckless in combining various types of plants if you expect your arrangement to live for some time. In one grouping, use shade-loving, heat-tolerant material; in another, plants which need sun and moisture; in a third, Succulents and Cacti which like sandy soil kept on the dry side. For an arrangement of bog plants, an area of open water in the center of a shallow dish will provide humidity, while the plants themselves, though kept moist, are protected from root rotting by the layer of drainage material under them.

Constructing the Arrangement

When the material and the container have been selected, and the drainage material and soil have been placed in the bottom, the arranger has several points which she must check carefully.

1. SCALE is of special importance here. In selecting plants, you may be tempted by a fine, large blooming or foliage plant. Before you use it, ask yourself whether you have a container which will hold the root ball comfortably and whether it is heavy enough to give this large specimen a suitable base. Next ask yourself whether the other plants available, or cut flowers, if these are to be used, are suitable in size and shape to go with it.

As in other arrangements, avoid using heavy-headed blooms with smaller ones at the base (as, for instance, Tulips with Grape-hyacinths). Instead, plant the base with a vine-like Myrtle or with moss or other ground cover which will not be dwarfed by the large blooms above.

Dainty miniatures of Crocuses, Squills, rock-garden Daffodils, and species Tulips are most appealing, but it is better to preserve a sense of scale by using these tiny flowers together.

2. LINE. The taller plants provide the silhouette and give the main lines of the design. Select these carefully and prune them if necessary to give the right effect. Seedling evergreens, Blueberries, and others can often be used to good advantage.

3. FOCAL INTEREST. In selecting the mass of color to be placed low in a living-plant arrangement for focal interest, you will want low-growing material with somewhat showy blooms or interesting shapes. Since these will form an important part of the arrangement, give them careful thought. African-violets are good because they give both color in the blooms, which last an exceptionally long time, and a definite rosette-like design in the plant. Echeverias in gray-green, red, or silver-gray, may be as effective as Roses. Cryptanthus is another rosette-like plant interesting in form and rich in its color combinations.

4. CAMOUFLAGE. When the plants have been set firmly in the soil, it is often necessary to cover the soil surface to pull the composition together and give it a natural look. It is easy to keep material on hand for this purpose or to gather it in the wild or in your own garden. A pot of Baby's Tears in the

window garden or the greenhouse is most useful for this camouflage work. Moss and lichens from the woods or Myrtle and
Moneywort from the garden are easy to get. At seasons when
ground covers are in bloom outdoors, a turf from one of these
may be cut and pressed into service.

Types of Living-Plant Arrangements

FOR SUN AND DRY AIR. Combine succulents and Cacti, using
a sandy mixture and keep only moderately damp.

Try the gray-green "roses" of an Echeveria as a focal center
for the bizarre lines of a tall *Kalanchoe tomentosa;* use a red
Echeveria rosette to emphasize the tortuous branches of a
Crown of Thorns with its blood-red blossoms at the tips.

Kalanchoe blossfeldiana cuttings bloom freely when only a
few inches tall. Plant several of these at the base of one of
the tall, slender succulents. The rosettes of the Gasterias and
Haworthias are also decorative enough to use for focal interest.

Cacti of various types grouped in a tray of sand are fascinating in the contrasts and harmonies of color, form, and texture.
Perhaps we are getting away from actual arrangement here
and sliding into the field of indoor gardening, but a skillful
artist can make such a collection into an arrangement which is
a thing of real beauty.

Geraniums in variety also offer rich possibilities for plants
which like to be kept a little on the dry side while they enjoy
sunshine and warmth. Look over the field of Scented, Ivy-
leaved, and Zonal Geraniums for really exciting material. The
foliage of many of these is more decorative than the blooms,
and by crushing a leaf one may scent a whole room delight-
fully. Rock plants which are not too rare to risk digging up can
also be utilized in this class.

FOR MOIST SHADE. The material for such a condition is
unlimited, as you will realize if you visit the "stove houses"
of a botanic garden or commercial grower and see the wealth
of small-leaved vines and other plants which revel in a jungle
atmosphere. African-violets can always be counted on for

Arrangement by Mrs. John R. Bear

A combination of small growing plants with larger cut branches gives the effect of a living arrangement.

color; or use Primulas instead (not the florists' types, but garden varieties, forced indoors).

Select a few small, colorful foliage plants at the florist and put them together about a miniature pool in an open dish. Maranta, *Ficus pumila,* green or in its variegated form, Philodendron, Crotons, Fittonias—the list is endless. To give such plants long life, use a terrarium or bring down from the attic the "bell glass" under which Grandmother kept her wax flowers or her stuffed squirrel. I often mourn the fact that I once refused the gift of a stuffed squirrel under glass. How useful that case would be if I had said yes!

Our own wild flowers offer excellent material: a Hemlock seedling for height and a tiny Maple for a touch of red foliage; Bank Violets and Marsh-marigolds against a rock or a bit of lichened tree root. Insert tiny Ferns and Partridge-berry in a mossy foreground. In another group, depend entirely on the fascinating forms and colors of the Pitcher-plant with Pixie-moss to cover the soil surface. By going out a week or two in advance of bloom and bringing in budded plants, you can force a wild-flower arrangement indoors. The simple beauty of a clump of Hepaticas against a gray miniature rock is hard to surpass.

FLOWERING PLANTS. Impatiens, *Begonia semperflorens* in variety, Fuchsias, and Exacum are a few of the good old reliable flowering plants which can be used in combination with foliage plants and ground covers for living-plant arrangements.

BULBS. Bulbs offer the greatest opportunities in the field of living-plant arrangements. All sorts can be used, from the showy tender ones like Amaryllis to spring-flowering kinds like Daffodils and Tulips, together with the dainty "minors" such as Muscari and Crocus. Bulbs like Paper-white Narcissus and Lily-of-the-valley, which force in pebbles or fiber, are easy to arrange because there is no problem of unsightly soil.

For late winter and early spring, force tender bulbs indoors and spring-flowering sorts in the usual manner by keeping them in a trench or cold cellar outdoors at freezing temperature and then bringing gradually to light, heat, and bloom.

By using a metal box, like a small window box, wonderful effects can be had with such tender bulbs as Amaryllis, Callas, and Veltheimia. Give the dormant bulb the place of honor in the box, where its straight spike lends height and dominates the picture. Around it plant foliage plants like Dracaena,

Arrangement by Mrs. John Potter

Small ferns and other plants with some roots attached
(even if without soil) will remain fresh for many days.

Birds-nest Fern, or large-leaved Begonias. The height can
taper down at the far end of the box to low-growing things
like Picka-back Plant, or Mother-of-thousands (*Saxifraga
sarmentosa*).

When your French Roman Hyacinths have come into bloom
in their pebbles or soil, set them off with a clump of Pansies

or a blooming African-violet. Paper-whites can be treated in the same way.

As for the spring-flowering bulbs, just think what you have to choose from. Such combinations as these suggest themselves: Squills and late white Crocuses; species Tulips and white Narcissi, set off with Myrtle, in bloom if you are lucky. Or plant yellow Crocuses and late Snowdrops in one dish, or yellow Crocuses and Chionodoxas. Use Kenilworth-ivy, German-ivy, Grape-ivy, Pothos, or *Ficus pumila variegata* to conceal the earth when you make a living-plant arrangement of bulbs. Nestle a clump of *Campanula carpatica* or a turf of creeping Phlox at the base of a group of white Tulips.

HERBS FOR SCENT. Sweet-scented herbs, such as Scented Geraniums, can be used for novel living-plant arrangements which have the added attraction of their aroma. These can be used alone or combined with other plant material.

Tender shrubs like Rosemary, Lemon-verbena, and Lavender are excellent to give height and line effects. Creeping Thyme is an excellent ground cover.

Place a clump of Colchicums at the base of a well-shaped Germander plant; or a Viola plant in full bloom with a graceful, sweet-scented Rosemary. White English Daisies and *Pelargonium crispa variegata* make a perfect combination.

Living-plant arrangements are something pleasant to think about and plan for. As plants come to your attention in the garden, the greenhouse, or the wild, their possibilities can be weighed and combinations made as the inspiration comes to you.

Even more exciting is to plant with a future arrangement in mind, placing tender bulbs with foliage plants for instance, and awaiting the miracle of the coming bloom. Or force your Paper-whites, Soleil d'ors, French Roman Hyacinths, or Lilies-of-the-valley in containers large enough to hold some low-growing accessory plant material when the bulbs come into bloom.

List of Plants for Living-Plant Arrangements

FLOWERING

Bulbs

Amaryllis
Calla-lily (dwarf)
Chionodoxas
Colchicum
Crocus
Daffodils (in variety)

Grape-hyacinths
Hyacinths, French Roman
Lily-of-the-valley
Scillas
Snowdrops
Tulips (in variety)

For Dry Heat and Sun

Cacti in variety
Succulents:
  Ceropegia
  Crassulas
  Cryptanthus
  Echeverias
  Euphorbia splendens

Gasterias
Haworthias
Kalanchoe blossfeldiana
Kalanchoe tomentosa
Sedums

Tall

Abelia (rooted cuttings)
Azaleas (small)
Begonia semperflorens
Browallia
Exacum
Fuchsias
Geraniums
Heliotrope (small)

Impatiens
Iris (dwarf)
Jerusalem Cherry (small)
Lantana
Pepper (decorative)
Phlox divaricata
Primulas (florists')
Tibouchina (small)

Low

African-violet
Campanula isophylla
Campanula carpatica
English Daisy
Myosotis
Myrtle

Oxalis
Pansies
Primulas (garden)
Roses, Pixie
Saxifraga sarmentosa
Violas

FOLIAGE

Tall

Crassula arborescens
Chinese Water Plant

Dracaena
Nephythytis (small)

Dwarf or Creeping

Baby's Tears
Coleus
Columnea
Crotons
Ferns
Ficus pumila
Fittonia
German-ivy
Grape-ivy
Hedera helix small-leaved
Kenilworth-ivy

Lichens
Marantas
Mosses
Myrtle
Pellionia
Peperomias
Philodendron
Picka-back Plant
Pileas
Saxifraga sarmentosa
Tradescantia

Herbs

Geraniums, Scented
Germander
Lemon-verbena (small)
Mint, Pineapple

Rosemary
Thyme, Creeping
Others

WILDLINGS

Anemones
Blueberry seedlings
Bluets
Columbine
Creeping Jenny
Cypripediums
Deciduous tree seedlings
Dutchman's Breeches
Evergreen seedlings
Ferns
Foamflower
Hepatica
Jack-in-the-pulpit
Lichens

Lycopodiums
Marsh-marigold
Mosses
Orchids, in variety
Partridgeberry
Pipsissewa
Rattlesnake-plantain
Spring Beauties
Star Flower
Troutlilies
Twinflowers
Violets
Wintergreen

CHAPTER XXI

Arrangements to Wear

BY NATALIE BOWEN

A form of flower arrangement which could well become more popular among women who enjoy working with cut flowers is that of making at home individual, interesting corsages, bouquets, and garlands to wear for personal adornment. Making corsages at home doesn't rule out the thrill of a Gardenia or an Orchid in a white florist's box. Far from it. But it does mean that a girl isn't wholly dependent upon getting one in order to give her best dress and her spirits the festive air that comes from wearing fresh flowers.

Then, too, there's the other side of the picture. As any man has found out (if he's worth his salt), buying flower ornaments is an item that can run into real money. So it's good to know that he (God forbid) or the woman in the case can make a corsage more original than and quite as charming as the one the florist makes, and for far less than he charges you for doing it. It's really a simple matter. A few flowers, a few ideas, some simple supplies, and a knack that is partly know how and partly a little practice, are all you need.

The economy and the satisfaction of using flowers fresh from your own garden are easy to see. But even during the winter months it is much cheaper to buy just a few flowers of your own choice and make up your own ornaments than simply to order ready-made corsages. Or given (?) the cut flowers, and after placing them in arrangements around the house, you could save out two or three blossoms to make into a little corsage for yourself or for a friend to whom you wish to send some thoughtful personal remembrance. Charming party favors, made simply and inexpensively yourself from fresh flowers, add a lot to your reputation as a thoughtful and original hostess.

Last and best of all, making corsages is a lot of fun. It gives you a chance to let your imagination carry your fingers where it will and allows you to use flowers which are lovely yet seldom used by florists for corsages because they are scarce, or hard to ship well, or expensive to raise commercially. You have no such restrictions and can choose any flower, cultivated or wild, that ordinarily keeps well in water. Naturally you would avoid such delicate blossoms as, for example, the Moonflower, which wilts a few minutes after picking. The only essential rule is to let your flowers stand in deep, cold water for several hours before working.

The florist supplies you need for a really good job are: florist wire in three or four different gauges (Nos. 22, 24, and 27 are the ones most frequently used); a roll of parafilm or floral tape; corsage pins; and, if you like, chenille wires—which are simply glorified pipe cleaners dyed in various colors. Other items which you can probably unearth around the house include a sharp knife, wire cutter, scissors, Scotch tape, and ribbon (1). The florist supplies you can buy inexpensively and in small quantities at any friendly local florist shop. They are not available elsewhere, as the sources handling them are strictly wholesale trade stores.

As to method, there are just two essential tricks you need to master: *wiring* and *taping*. These you can practice on left-over flowers from your house bouquets or on spare flowers from the garden until you can do the job neatly. Then you are ready to tackle any flower you wish to wear.

There are two main ways of wiring and taping flowers for corsages, and which one you use depends on the kind of flower you are working with. Flowers with a heavy calyx, such as Roses, Carnations, Marigolds, should have the stems cut off quite close to the flower head. The less stem you leave, the

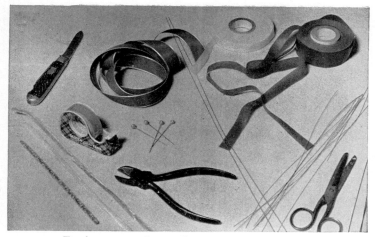

1. Equipment and supplies.

neater your work will be. The wire is pulled through the calyx, twisted once or twice below, and then the wire and what is left of the stem are neatly covered with parafilm. Start the tape slightly below the point where the wire shows; firm it well with your fingers until it sticks, then twirl the stem, bringing the tape neatly up to a point above the wire and then all the way down to the length of finished stem you want. Hold the tape in one hand and twirl the stem with the other. With Roses (2) the head is broken from the stem entirely and wired, bringing both ends of the wire down to twist together before taping. With lighter flowers you could leave the wire single, twisting the short end higher up around the long one.

Next photograph (3) shows the second step in preparing a Rose. Here a single leaf from a Grape-ivy (a smart, practical substitute for Rose foliage, as it is more lasting) has been attached with a bit of No. 27 wire and is being taped along with the Rose stem. Wire and tape all Rose blossoms and buds, add the foliage (allowing about three leaves to a medium-sized corsage), and then assemble the whole. To appreciate fully the finished product, think first of the typical "subway corsage"— the kind you see sold at subway stands and by run-of-the-mill

2. *Severed Rose being "wired."*

florists. It consists of Roses which are all laid together, wired along with their own foliage and backed with some Asparagus-fern, and the rough ends of the wires camouflaged with silver tinsel ribbon.

To make matters even worse, the florist will often pin it on your coat with the Rose heads down so that the ribbon shows

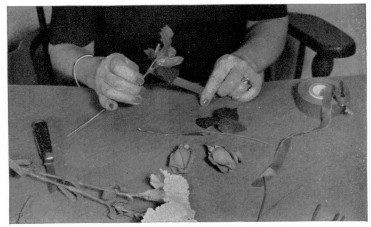

3. *Foliage (Grape-ivy) is added.*

4. Corsages—homemade and commercial.

most of all. Here, on the contrary, is a corsage (4) such as you could make for yourself, using the same type and number of Roses—for example, three semi-open ones and two buds. These are wired and taped with two leaves of Grape-ivy and separated into two clusters, with three Roses going one way and two the other. The two clusters are wired and taped in the middle, the joining is neatly taped, and the Roses are bent in a graceful design. (One of the main reasons for wiring and

5. Method of wiring flowers with shallow calyx—such as Blue Lace-flower.

6. A single wire is pushed up through calyx, then bent into hook and pulled back.

taping is that you can bend the stems to assume a graceful line.) This corsage does not need any ribbon. It can be worn any way—up, down, at the shoulder, waist, or in the hair.

Flowers with a wide head and very shallow calyx, such as pompon Chrysanthemums, Daisies, Blue Lace-flower (5), need a different method of wiring. The straight wire is pushed up from the bottom through the head of the flower and the end bent into a tiny hook. Then the wire is gently pulled back

7. Bracelet of Roses, with matching ribbon.

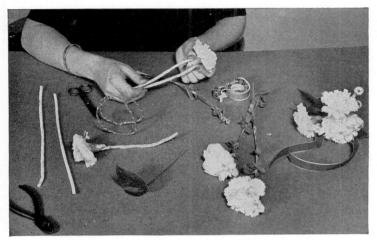

8. *Making a bracelet; foundation is formed of three wires taped together, bent to fit wrist.*

so that the hook will be invisible (6) and the flower head securely attached to the wire.

The first step in making a cluster or "Colonial" bouquet is to remove the stems entirely and wire the flowers as described earlier. Do not tape them yet, however, but assemble the flowers, securely wired, into the design you have in mind. When the whole is complete, twist one wire around *all* the stems, and

9. *Proof of the pudding—various types of corsages.*

239

10. Floral shoulder strap, neckpiece, and comb.

tape them all together. (These same flowers when used for any other type of corsage would need taping, as shown in the photographs.)

For these Colonial corsages it's pretty to use a border of leaves or a paper lace doily holder. For these photographs we used the leaves from a plant of *Cissus antarctica*. Galax leaves or Ivy would also be very effective. Speaking of leaves, we would like to suggest that you use foliage from your house plants or your garden rather than anything resembling florist Fern, which looks really well with only a few flowers. Many corsages need no foliage at all, but some are enhanced by the use of Pittsburgh Ivy, Grape-ivy, Pothos, Philodendron, Cissus, Geranium, or any other interesting leaf you can spare from your plants.

A flower wristlet like the finished one shown, of red Roses with Grape-ivy foliage and red velvet ribbon to match the flowers (7), or the bracelet being made with white Carnations (8), is made as follows: Take three No. 20 or 22 wires long enough to go twice around your wrist. Tape them together, join to make a circle, and then bend to make an open double circle (as shown directly under the right hand, 8). Cover the taped wire with ribbon to match or contrast with the flower, as you choose, and use Scotch tape to fasten the ribbon over the wire frame at the start and finish of the ribbon-winding operation. If you use Roses, prepare them exactly as you would for a Rose corsage and fasten them with wire and tape to the wire bracelet. Bend the bracelet to fit your wrist securely. If you use Carnations, follow the steps shown in photograph 8. Here the Carnations are broken off their stems, chenille wire is pulled through the calyx, and one short end is securely twisted around the long end. These chenille-wired flowers are secured to the bracelet, and the ends of chenille can be curlicued to resemble tendrils. A ribbon bow finishes the bracelet, and no foliage is necessary unless you think one leaf of Philodendron, shown wired and taped (8), helps to complete the design.

Now, as proof of the pudding, so to speak, take a look at six finished corsages (9), any of which, or others similar, you could easily make yourself after a little practice. Top row, left to right: red Carnations wired on chenille, with Cissus foliage; three open Gladiolus blossoms and two small buds, each wired separately and joined to very small tip leaves of Rhododendron; a cluster bouquet of Daisies, Pansies, Sweet Peas, Blue Laceflower, having a Sweetheart Rose for the center, a border of Cissus foliage, and finished with two looped ends of ribbon. Bottom row: bronze and yellow pompon Chrysanthemums in close arrangement, without foliage, held by pale green ribbon tied not in bows but in several straight double ends and left hanging; small clusters of Violets and Daisies, with Galax foliage; a Colonial bouquet of yellow Pompons and deep maroon and orange Marigolds, with Cissus foliage and yellow ribbon bow.

Experiment, too, with arranging flowers on a comb especially for your hair, or on a ribbon to wear around your neck or over one shoulder with a strapless evening gown. Photograph 10 shows you an example of each: a comb with pompon Chrysanthemums and Pittsburgh Ivy wired on; a wide shoulder strap of velvet ribbon with three Carnations wired on curlicued chenille and clustered at the shoulder, and a single Carnation each at front and back where the ribbon joins the gown; a narrower velvet ribbon to wear around the neck with a cluster of Sweetheart Roses wired on pendant fashion, and a single Rosebud at either side. With any of these you prepare flowers as for corsages and then wire them onto ribbon or comb. Be careful, with the latter, to tuck in the wire ends so that they won't catch in your hair. Other than that, there's no problem whatever. The idea and method are basic, the varieties as infinite as flowers, style of dress, and your own ingenuity will allow.

Part Three

PLANT MATERIALS FOR ARRANGEMENTS

Arrangements by Miss Mildred Sawyer and by Mrs. George Green (below)

FOR CUTTING

In planting your garden, provide a succession of flowers especially good for arrangements. Excellent for spring are any of the Poets Narcissi; for autumn, Dahlia Bishop of Llandaff.

CHAPTER XXII

Cut Flowers—To Buy; to Grow

From the Florist

If and when you buy florists' flowers, it is sensible to know something about what should be available in the market at the time. Consult the list in Chapter XXVI and note what is seasonal. After a little experience you will learn the price range, and manage somehow to content yourself with what you can afford. If Roses are $20 a dozen, Snapdragons and Iris may have to do. But of course the price of Roses—and other flowers too—varies with the season and even with growing conditions in that particular season. The wholesalers try to grow crops to mature for the big holidays, and "special" days (like Mother's Day), and if cloudy weather or other difficulties hold them back so that they miss their objective, the market may be glutted with Roses or Carnations or Gladiolus a week after Christmas or Memorial Day or some other special season. It is then that you can buy first-class cut flowers very cheaply. It is wise to ask your florist to inform you when such gluts occur. You may be able to profit by them.

And that brings us to the florist. It pays to deal with one reliable firm. If you can find a good man in a convenient spot, give him your regular trade. If you are a good planner, you will decide several days in advance what flowers you want and, after ascertaining about what they will cost, order them. Give him a second choice, in case he fails to find the original flowers selected.

Discuss your decoration problems with him too. Tell him how much your budget allows for flowers and ask him to keep you informed of any special bargains which he thinks might interest you. Above all, in the beginning establish the fact that you must have *fresh* flowers at all times—that stale material sold to you as fresh will result at once in your taking your trade elsewhere.

By establishing permanent and intelligent relations with your florist, you have a real ally—one who knows flowers, who can tell you how long each should last, and who can often suggest substitutes when what you want is not to be had.

When ordering flowers, it is also wise to ask for a green which may be usable in your arrangement. Asparagus Fern almost never is desirable. Huckleberry, Galax, Smilax, Laurel, Rhododendron, and autumn leaves are sometimes helpful. Even if you have to pay a few cents extra to get the right green, it is better to buy what you can use.

What to Buy

Among the most reliable cut flowers—those which give the most show and longest life for their price—are Gladiolus and Snapdragons, which can start out in tall vases and be cut down as they lose their lower florets until they end in low vases or as floating arrangements. These two flowers, being grown in many parts of the country the year round, are never prohibitively high in price. When Snapdragons are not satisfactory or available to give height to your bouquets, substitute Stocks, Heather, or Stephanotis. Chrysanthemums are probably the longest lasting of any florists' flower, with the possible exception of Mimosa, which dries without losing form and color. Some of the small-flowered Mums do almost the same thing.

First-quality Carnations are long-lasting also, but for just that reason they are often sold after they have passed their prime. Be sure your Carnations are fresh; if they seem suspiciously cheap in price, beware!

Roses are always high-priced, but for arrangements, medium or even short-stemmed grades often are better than "firsts" *if* they are fresh.

Sweet Peas and Freesias are short-lived, but are deliciously fragrant.

For modern compositions Strelitzias, Tritomas, Foxtail-lilies, Anthuriums, Nerines, Callas, Amaryllis, and other true Lilies of many sorts are often available. At least some of these can be had at any time of year.

For the table, select Orchids, Camellias, or Gardenias if your taste is exotic or, if simple, Gerberas, Carnations, or Roses.

Don't forget the gay pageant of forced bulbous flowers when planning arrangements for late winter and early spring. To go with them, Lilac and less expensive forced shrubs like Pussywillow or blooming fruit branches are sometimes available.

Planting for Arrangement Material

Plan in advance to provide yourself with flowers and foliage grown especially for making arrangements.

The advantages of making at least a few plantings, especially for arrangement material, are many. You can provide just the *colors* you want—to go with each other, or to suit the surroundings they will have. You can get dominating flower *forms* —bold ones for focal points of interest, tall spikes to keep arrangements from being squatty, and sprays that will add gracefulness to bouquets of more substantial blooms.

And last, but by no means least, you will be assured a *continuity* of arrangement material that can never be attained when you merely cut hit or miss among your garden borders of annuals, perennials, bulbs, and shrubs.

A Cutting Garden

You can save space, time, and work by putting these selected plants in a special cutting garden by themselves—and grow better flowers! If you've a vegetable patch, a few short rows there devoted to a couple of dozen annuals, perennials, and bulbs will yield a most surprising crop of choice arrangement material.

An alternate plan is to put enough favorite plants in the beds and border so that any cut blossoms will not be missed. This is our method at GrayRock.

In the seasons of maximum bloom we can cut bucketfuls of flowers from the borders without causing a gap in the color mass. And while cutting, I snip off dead blossoms, look for insects, and pull large weeds. We do have a cutting bed, too, down by the gate to the lower vegetable garden. It is not on general show, but is so colorful that guests usually want to walk down to get a closer view.

Among the species and varieties which we have found particularly useful a number are suggested in the following paragraphs. Unless you have a large garden, you will not want to attempt all of them, especially the first year. But selections from among them will give you a good start toward more dependable material for summer arrangements.

ANNUALS. Among Petunias, the new Mrs. Dwight D. Eisenhower and Rose Marie are very satisfactory for cutting. Our favorite white is the lovely Lace Veil, a large fringed flower on rather low, compact plants. We like Cheerful (light salmon-pink), Igloo (white), and Blue Bird; Hollywood Star is distinctive in form. Of the Marigolds, Limelight, Mayling, and Buff Beauty are pastel colors which combine well with blue, purple, and lavender flowers.

For smaller bouquets *Phlox drummondi* Salmon Glory and the old favorite Isabellina, a soft primrose buff, are most useful. So also are Verbenas, which bloom until hard frost and offer fine colors and graceful flower heads for use with Roses and other flowers. Lavender Glory, Floradale Beauty, and Apple Blossom are choice.

The small Bedding Dahlias and Coltness Hybrids (which can be started from seed indoors and grown as annuals) provide an amazing range of color and form for cutting. China Asters come into blossom fairly late and give large, showy blooms of pale, delicate colors at a time when these are scarce. Select wilt-resistant strains.

For red, orange, and gold, frail-stemmed blooms to be placed in metal containers, don't forget the good old Calliopsis and the newer yellow and orange Cosmos varieties. Anemone-flowered Cosmos, in red, pink, and white, tufted in the center, give an out-of-the-ordinary note.

Other annuals for the cutting garden are Zinnias in variety; Mignonette, for fragrance; Salpiglossis, for the delicate blue or red gold-veined, trumpet-shaped blooms; double scented Nasturtiums; Nigella, to give pure sky-blue accents; Calendula Art Shades or Pastel Shades, for soft buffs and creamy golds; and Snapdragons, for height and a fine color range.

To Give Height. Snapdragons are indispensable to the arranger of flowers because of their brilliant colors, graceful spikes, and long period of bloom. In order to have them very early, we carry mature plants over winter in a frame. These blossom bravely when set out until the seedlings, started in February in the greenhouse, are ready to take over. Pinks, reds, and whites I use in combination with other flowers of these colors, and with blue. Oranges, salmons, and yellows go well with coarser things like Zinnias and Calendulas, and also with many bicolor Roses. When procuring seeds of Snapdragons, it is always safer to select rust-resistant varieties.

Other annuals which give airy height in mixed arrangements are white and pale pink Larkspurs and the Chinese Larkspur (*Delphinium Chinense*) in various shades of blue; Cynoglossums in blue and white; Anchusa; Mignonette, and Salvia Blue Bedder or *farinacea*.

Flowers Which Stand Alone. For graceful, light bouquets all made up of one variety or of several varieties of the same species, we like the double-crested Cosmos Pink Lady and White Cloud in combination; great crimson Sensation Cosmos Dazzler in a red cordial bottle or a white pottery jar; and yellow, orange, or golden Cosmos combined in a pewter and copper vase.

Petunias lend themselves to use alone or with other flowers. We are fond of line arrangements made from a few branches of Glamour or Theodosia.

Another flower which can well be used alone is Tithonia or Mexican Sunflower. The single, broad-petaled blooms are brilliant red-orange and the foliage is interestingly laciniated. It grows so tall, however, that we often screen the compost heap with a dozen plants. Orange Calendulas in a deep blue pottery pitcher; Nasturtiums and leaves in a brown or yellow jug; great Goldsmith or Yellowstone Marigolds massed in a copper water jar, and Super Crown o' Gold Pastel Tints Zinnias (ranging in color from pale buff through primrose to gold, salmon, and deep rose) in a carved Chinese soapstone container are other favorites for one-flower arrangements.

PERENNIALS. Some of these can be grown from seed, others must be purchased as plants, but all are worth while.

The large-flowered garden Carnations, with their long flowering season, are especially useful. Old Spice (salmon pink), Westwood Beauty (crimson), and Marie Chabaud (pale yellow) are some of our favorites. Except for Old Spice, these can be raised at home from seed.

For easily made one-, two-, or three-flower line arrangements in low Oriental dishes, have a group of single and semi-double Peonies in white, shell-pink, and pale yellow. Especially effective are Oriental Poppies, which, if the stem ends are seared and the flowers properly hardened in water after cutting, last well.

For autumn arrangements you will want lots of Hardy Chrysanthemums in your favorite colors. Include Lavender Lady, Burgundy (red), and Magnolia, an exquisite rosy buff with wheat tones.

In Iris, Siberian, Japanese, and Bulbous types are all much better for cut flowers than the more commonly grown Bearded ones. The yellow-flowered, moisture-loving *Iris pseudacorus* is particularly good.

SPRING BULBS. When ordering your next lot of hardy bulbs, choose some of the white and creamy Daffodils like John Evelyn, Gertie Millar, and Beersheba for flower compositions which will be as chastely beautiful as any made from Lilies, Freesias, Gardenias, or other exotic florists' flowers. The dainty little fellows like Agnes Harvey and Moonshine are lovely for small line arrangements. Combine them with Chionodoxas or Grape-hyacinths. Go over the Tulip lists carefully, too, and select a few of medium height in colors and forms especially suitable for cut-flower work. These make very distinguished arrangements combined with Lilacs and other spring flowers, or they can be effectively arranged alone.

SUMMER BULBS. Have a row of the informal Primulinus hybrid Gladiolus in your cutting garden. Two or three plantings will provide a succession of blooms from July to frost. These are much easier to arrange than the usual large-flowered kinds such as most gardeners plant.

And when ordering garden Lilies, add some extra bulbs to grow for cut flowers. *Lilium speciosum rubrum* is one of the loveliest for arrangements and is easy to grow, as are *L. auratum, L. regale,* and *L. philippinense.* A summer bulb valuable for both the white flowers and glossy straplike foliage is the fragrant Amaryllis-like Ismene. The leaves can be used all summer as accessory foliage. If you grow Tuberous-rooted Begonias for brilliant color in the shade, these will double for Camellias in table arrangements. Remove the single flowers, leaving only the double center bloom. Cut as soon as fully open and harden in cool water. They provide good foliage, as do also the exotic Fancy-leaved Caladiums. Include also a few of the more unusual ones. Callas grow well in the open, and for a real exotic, try the gorgeous red-and-yellow Gloriosa.

SHRUBS. Valuable arrangement material is to be found in the Hawthorns, flowering fruit trees, Philadelphus, Forsythia, Magnolias, Buddleias in variety, and even in the common high-bush Blueberry, whose flowers and autumn foliage are both excellent. *Viburnum triloba,* or Cranberry Bush, is another showy native with beautiful fall foliage and colorful fruit. Don't forget the usefulness of Rhododendron, Laurel, Andromeda, and other broad-leaved evergreens for flowers and foliage.

VINES. Wisteria is one of the choicest vines for cut-flower material. Foliage, tendrils, and flowers are all graceful and desirable. Then, too, there are many Clematis varieties in white, pink, and purple. The common small-flowered Virgins Bower (*Clematis virginiana*) and Travelers Joy (*C. vitalba*) can be utilized in flower, and later in seed. Bittersweet is worth growing in the home garden to provide dried material.

Of annual vines, *Cobaea scandens* is perhaps the most unique. It is commonly known as Cup-and-saucer Vine. Plant this against the house in sun or shade. Watch it climb to the roof, and in late summer and fall cut its showy single Canterbury Bell-like blue flowers, flower-like calyxes, decorative foliage, and wiry tendrils for distinctive line arrangements or for use in mixed mass compositions.

Another vine which we always have around our kitchen door, and growing up to the open deck above, is the Moonflower (planted with Heavenly Blue Morning Glory). This is a valuable annual for dinner-table arrangements. We bring in the tips of vines and leaves during the day and arrange them in a low bubble-glass dish. Then, just before dinner—about seven o'clock—when the great fragrant blooms are opening, we clip flowers with enough stem to carry them above the water in the dish. They remain open and disseminate fragrance throughout the evening.

FOLIAGE. Most amateurs fail to realize the importance of available good foliage to supplement their flowers in making arrangements. Hostas, Coleus, a plant of Variegated Ivy, will work wonders in adding distinction to your indoor decorations.

We usually also have at least a few plants of silver-gray *Leucophae candicans* and *Cineraria maritima*. For large arrangements, small leaves of the Castor Oil Bean are good (and don't fail to use the seed pods, too, when they develop). Of course there is always Canna foliage and, in our garden at least, there usually can be found a rosette of Giant Mullein foliage, spared for the purpose.

Cutting for Arrangements Gives More Bloom

Many annuals just won't go on blooming and giving of their colorful beauty unless they are cut and cut hard.

From the time the Pansies are set out in the early spring garden beds until frost threatens the last fall annuals and perennials, we gardeners are faced with the necessity of keeping seeds from forming on blooming plants in order to prolong the blossoming periods, or in some cases to assure a later second blooming. If an annual or a second-year biennial succeeds in setting a good crop of seeds, its work in the world, from its own point of view, is done, and it can die in peace. Cutting the faded blooms from perennials saves their strength for more bloom instead of expending it in an effort to set unwanted seeds.

Sweet Peas, like Pansies, are an outstanding example of flowers which must be constantly cut to keep them blooming. Many people these days find it hard to grow Sweet Peas successfully, but those who do know that for a long blossoming season the blooms must be cut in quantity every day.

In the case of many border plants, such well-loved ones as Sweet Alyssum, *Myosotis scorpiodes semperflorens* (true Forget-me-not), Cheiranthus (Siberian Wallflower), and dwarf

Phlox drummondi, which show masses of color and then continue to bloom, becoming more and more leggy as the flower stems lengthen and bearing faded blooms on the lower portions and fresh flowers at the tips of the stems, it is necessary to harden your heart. Before this condition goes too far, shear off the lengthening, straggly blooming stems. Surprisingly soon the plants will put out new growth.

Petunia is another annual which cannot be permitted to straggle and lop indefinitely just because fresh flowers continue to appear at the tips of its vine-like branches. Cut back the fringed double and larger single types, a branch or two at a time, before they get out of hand; otherwise some morning after a rain you will look out of the window to find your magnificent Petunia border has suddenly collapsed and resembles a twisted mass of green wires in which faded bits of colored cloths have been entangled. The dwarf Gem type, however, needs no pruning.

Clip off faded blossoms of all garden flowers. In the case of hardy annuals which may self-seed, or when you wish to save seed for replanting, let one or a few especially fine plants go to seed, and take good care of the seeds by drying and storing them in a dry place.

Delphinium is one of the perennials which can be counted on for a second blooming period if the dead flower spikes are carefully removed after spring flowering. Perennial Phlox, which blooms for a much longer period, is encouraged to keep up the good work by having faded blooms removed, and this practice also prevents the nuisance of self-seeding with its resultant plants of dirty cerise or faded purplish rose.

Since late-blooming perennials, like Asters and Chrysanthemums, are likely to be cut down by frost rather than stopped by seed formation, the removal of faded flowers is important for neatness rather than for prolongation of bloom. With early-flowering varieties, however, like those which start in August or early September, cutting dead flower heads will help the plants to show masses of color until killing frost.

Roses, most of which nowadays give some bloom each

month, need particular care to prevent seeding. Removing the old flowers is necessary first of all to keep the Rose garden beautiful and to discourage pests; second, if maximum bloom is expected, the plants must not waste their energy in seed making.

Bulbs, even those which blossom only once a year, like Tulips and Daffodils, will have larger and better flowers the following season if dead flowers are removed to prevent seeding. Since the plant is working from blossomtime until its rest period, when foliage dies back, to store within its bulb the embryo of next year's flower, it is unwise to have it put part of its strength into undesired and unneeded seed making.

So when you come in from the garden with a great basket of cut flowers, ready to decorate the house, do not feel that you are robbing the garden beds. On the contrary, you are assuring continued and better bloom.

Forced Shrub Branches for Late Winter Indoors

Grace Coyle, whose name you know as an arranger and writer, gives these hints on another source of garden material for cutting.

"Along in February do you feel that you have had all the winter you can take? Do you look out at the bare branches of shrubs and trees against a gray sky and wonder how you can survive until you see them clothed in beauty once more?

"Don't wait. Bring some of those twigs into the house and force them, or, to be more polite, encourage them. 'Encourage' means to help forward, and so is not only less rude but more appropriate.

"Watch for a day when the temperature is above freezing, then gather your twigs of Apple, Pear, and Cherry; Peach, Plum, and Flowering Quince; Forsythia and Bridal Wreath (*Spirea prunifolia*). But the twigs must not be too 'twiggy.'

They should be of at least finger thickness where cut from the shrub or tree in order to furnish enough nourishment for them to develop new growth.

"Bruise and shred the stem ends of branches for about two inches by pounding with a hammer. This seemingly cruel process causes them to take up water more readily. If the branches are to be used in flower arrangements, by all means prune and shape them as nearly as possible to the heart's desire before encouraging (or forcing) starts, as performing these operations when the twigs are covered with frail young leaves and blossoms is indeed nerve-racking.

"Stand the branches in rather deep water, using a vase or jar which holds not less than a quart and more if possible. Whether the container is transparent or opaque seems to make no difference. In the living room, even at sixty-five degrees, it is better to place them five or six feet from a south window where they will get the sun's influence rather than the direct rays. Never stand them near a radiator. Comparative coolness gives the young leaves and blossoms firmer texture. However, unless you have greenhouse conditions, do not expect the forced blossoms to have quite the brilliance of color that they would attain out of doors.

"For early forcing, Winter Jasmine (*Jasminum nudiflorum*), Forsythia, Alder, Spicebush (*Lindera benzoin*), and Pussywillow are especially suitable.

"Inasmuch as Forsythia is the most commonly seen forced material, it is a pleasant variation to combine these branches with other plants. A few twigs added to a pot of forced Narcissus or with branches of Alder, Pussywillow, or Pine cones, give a suitable springlike effect. The branches, clipped to the desired size, make a most attractive addition to a dish-garden arrangement.

"Bush Honeysuckle is desirable for forcing because of its fragrance. The Alder has little pendent catkins that are very interesting. Later on, branches of Peach, Apple, Plum, Flowering Quince, Cherry, Corylopsis, and Xanthorhiza are treasured for their delicate blossoms.

"Nor are blossoms the only beauty you may expect. Young fans of Horse-chestnut leaves on their strong, varnished stems, finely pleated Beech leaves, like tiny green flames, and even humble Gray Birch in its fresh green are things to be enjoyed in winter. And you will agree that there is nothing lovelier than rosy-silver young Oak leaves. Be patient with these twigs, however, as they will be the very last to open their leaf buds.

"In addition to the more frequently forced fruit blossoms and shrubs already mentioned try Mountain Ash (Sorbus), which is very beautiful and long-lasting. The delicacy of forced Japanese Maple is something to dream about, and if you can find a deciduous conifer (such as the Bald-cypress or one of the Larches), take a branch, with some of the little cones if possible. It is very easily encouraged, and when covered with fine pale jade needles you have a fairy thing. Barberry is not a lovable plant, but somehow, when encouraged indoors, it seems to take on a gentler nature and is really quite attractive.

"Any branch is beautiful clothing itself in new green, so cut it and bring it in. Encourage it, and it will help you forward into spring."

EFFECTIVE FOLIAGE

Arrangements by Mrs. Constance B. Wallace and Mrs. George A. Lofland

Here are two fine examples of flowerless flower arrangements— one composed of a rosette of Aloe, with ascending Sansevieria leaves; the other of Mullein and foliage of the Globe-thistle.

CHAPTER XXIII

Effective Foliage

Accessory foliage is a most important part of arrangement material and cannot be given too much consideration, whether you are growing it in the garden for this purpose, buying it from a florist, or keeping it in the window garden ready for use in the form of foliage plants.

In selecting it, the following attributes should be considered:

FORM. The shape of the leaves and growing habit of the plant.

COLOR. There is great variation here, from the white of fancy-leaved Caladium to the deep red of a Canna leaf or the forest green of a Rhododendron.

TEXTURE. Foliage can often be chosen to harmonize with the texture of the container: Broadleaf evergreens for glossy pottery or glass and for highly polished metal; Rex Begonia and other large-leaf Begonia leaves for hand-beaten metal, and so on.

It is not too hard to find interesting foliage, appropriate to each arrangement, and this is true even if no good florist is accessible.

Florists' Material

From the florist, for show arrangements and really impressive compositions for use at home, you can secure, by ordering in advance, glossy dark Magnolia leaves, Eucalyptus, *Pittosporum,* Cypress, and the foliage of Callas, Strelitzias, Arums, and Spathiphyllum. Leaves of the white-veined Fancy-leaved Caladiums are striking, as are also the colored forms. Sometimes such broadleaf evergreens as Photinia, Mahonia, Loquat, and Camellia are available.

Do not accept the useless Asparagus Fern, which is sent with most flowers. Ask for Huckleberry, Galax, or Smilax instead. In autumn all florists carry red Oak leaves. These may work into a fall arrangement and prove very useful indeed.

Most florists stock, in winter at least, Rhododendron and Laurel foliage, and often Pine and Cedar branches. These are helpful in making semi-permanent home arrangements to be used with successive lots of fresh flowers to give emphasis.

Toward spring you can order Pussywillows and branches of spring-flowering shrubs to work into arrangements of spring bulbs.

Botanical Gardens

For exhibition work, when something unique is required, it pays to visit a botanical garden, if one is within reach. Here, in the tropical houses, a wealth of material will present itself. Notes can be made on what is desired, and sometimes it can be obtained through a florist or commercial greenhouse. The consultant at the garden can often advise where a specific plant can be obtained.

A less sure but no less interesting method is to visit local greenhouse men. Even the most prosaic grower under glass usually has an Orange tree in the corner of one house or a tropical vine clinging to the ventilator rods overhead.

From the Garden

EVERGREENS. *Broadleaf evergreens* are a treasure house in that they store ever-ready accessory foliage until needed by the arranger. Plant your shrubs with this thought in mind. Be sure to have the real standbys, like Rhododendrons, Kalmias, evergreen Azaleas, Box, Holly, Abelia, Cotoneasters, Pyracanthas, Leucothoes, and Pieris. On the West coast this list is swelled by more lovely plants than we have space to name. Among them are Camellias, Mahonias, *Laurus nobilis* (Sweet Bay), Ceanothus, Magnolias, Nandina, Photinias, and Barberies.

Then, too, there are the *ground covers* and vines like Vinca *major* and *minor,* Pachysandra, and the Ivies, including small-leaved and variegated sorts.

CONIFEROUS EVERGREENS, and others like Cedar, Juniper, and Yew, make excellent arrangement material, especially if you are farsighted enough to plant dwarf varieties. It is usually difficult to cut a branch small enough from a White Pine or Hemlock. Dwarf growers, however, offer just what is required. Juniper berries cling indefinitely to the branches, making semi-permanent arrangement material which can hardly be excelled. Yew, in water, remains fresh and glossy for many weeks.

Select each branch carefully before cutting and be sure not to mar the shape of a slow-growing evergreen with a hasty pair of shears. Often it is possible to find a suitable branch near the ground where its removal does not show.

DECIDUOUS TREES, VINES, AND SHRUBS can be tapped to yield a rich harvest.

Purple Beech or Copper Beech is always popular. Tulip Tree and Sweet Gum have fascinating leaf forms. Japanese Maple, Mountain Ash, and Fig are outstanding for the beauty of their foliage.

Wisteria is perhaps the best vine of all for arrangement because of its graceful curving growth and interesting foliage, but there are others like Trumpet Creeper, Clematis in variety, and Climbing Hydrangea.

Shrubs like deciduous Azaleas, Tamarisk, the Viburnums, and the Dogwood are good too.

In the Garden

Common garden plants which are constantly used for accessory foliage in arrangement include Irises, Hostas (especially the variegated ones), Coleus, Cannas, red Amaranth, and Castor Oil Bean.

Many arrangers grow Globe Artichoke, Santolina, Stachys, Artemisias, *Leucophae candicans,* and *Cineraria maritima* in order to have gray-foliaged plants always available when needed.

Tender summer-flowering bulbs with straplike leaves, like Ismenes, Agapanthus, and Amaryllis, are invaluable, while the foliage from hardy bulbs—Daffodils, Hyacinths, Lily-of-the-valley, and *Lycoris squamigera*—are useful in season.

VEGETABLES. We must not forget that one of our famous English arrangers, Constance Spry, featured Kale leaves in bouquets and got plenty of publicity out of it, if not approval. And many a prize in a show has been won with a red cabbage and with Burpee's famous Rhubarb Chard. The heads of Leeks, Onions, and Chives, though they are flowers, not foliage, might be mentioned here also. Few materials are lovelier or longer lasting.

HERBS. The herb garden offers many sweet-scented foliage plants: Lemon Verbena and Rosemary—the latter especially for miniatures; and the bold leaves of Borage, Clary Sage, and Curly Tansy. Richest field of all is that of the scented Geraniums. No other leaf has the velvety quality of the Mint Geranium, *Pelargonium tomentosa.* Then there are the skeleton types (most of them rose-scented), the Oak Leafs, Zonals, and last but not least the small curly *P. crispa* and *P. crispa variegata,* lemon-scented.

HOUSE PLANTS offer another broad field for the arranger. Among the most useful are large-leaf Begonias, Monsteras,

*Arrangements by Mrs.
Erik A. Thomee and Mrs.
Janet K. Ferguson, Jr., and
by Richard M. Hurd*

*You may not care to
make arrangements of fo-
liage alone, but large, bold
leaves will add much to
your flower compositions.
Above are Dracaena
leaves with Cotyledon;
right, Strelitzia, Begonia,
and Cotyledon.*

Philodendrons, Dracaenas (especially the red-foliaged and spotted varieties), Dieffenbachias, Bird's-nest Fern, Calla leaves, Strelitzia leaves, Fancy-leaved Caladiums, Aspidistra, Fiddle-leaf Rubber Plant, Sansevieria, and Pandanus. And we must not forget the Ivies, including some of the variegated varieties. *Ficus pumila,* or Creeping Fig, has charming flat, roundish leaves and the vines curve gracefully as they grow against wall or trellis.

Succulents are much used, the rosette types often being substituted for flowers as centers of interest in all-green compositions. Many succulents bear spikes of charming flowers as well, and this is an extra dividend. Echeverias, Haworthias, and Gasterias have colorful, long-lasting blooms. Kalanchoes, Sempervivums, Cryptanthuses, and others are equally good, giving unique colors, color combinations, and forms.

WILD PLANTS can be drawn on also. Bear in mind the Great Mullein and even the humble Plantain, together with the foliage of Dogtooth Violets and Rattlesnake Plantain. Then, too, there are the water plants such as Arrowhead, and Waterlilies, with their round glossy leaves. The common Horsetail of the West is seen in many distinctive compositions.

Ferns are a host in themselves. Try Fiddleheads (the young curled unopened fronds) in early spring for line arrangements and dried fertile fronds in winter with other dried material. They have a grace all their own!

When purchasing seeds, plants, and shrubs for your garden, and house plants for winter rooms, keep arrangements in mind and select at least some material which can be counted on for accessory foliage. By so doing you will combine your dividends—garden beauty or permanent room decoration, plus foliage material which will be available when you need it for cut-flower work.

CHAPTER XXIV

Treasure Trove of Wild Flowers

From the moment in early spring when the Spice-bush shows its golden blossoms along bare branches to November when Witchhazel puts on her out-of-season display, there is a wealth of wild material to be had for the cutting, if conservation laws permit. Failing that permission, many people think it worth while to grow wildlings in their gardens for careful and prescribed cutting, since many of these make outstanding arrangement material.

SPRING-FLOWERING SHRUBS. This pageant, which starts with Pussywillow and Spicebush, continues with the Alders, bearing their charming catkins, the High-bush Blueberries, shaking their rosy bells, Dogwood, Honeysuckles, Viburnums, Chokecherries, and Shadblows (*Amelanchiers*).

In the West and parts of the South, the field is much richer, yielding Spiraeas, Ceanothus, Philadelphus, and the Crataeguses, among many others.

As the season advances, the broadleaf evergreens put on their show together with deciduous Azaleas. Among the most widely available are Rhododendrons, Laurels (Kalmias), and Leucothoes.

In the South or West, evergreen Ceanothus, Broom, Azaleas, Magnolias, Mahonias, Pieris, and Myrica (or Wax Myrtle) are added, to name but a few.

265

FLOWERING TREES. For really distinctive arrangements, try the flowers and foliage of the dignified Tulip Tree, the blooms and foliage of Catalpa, and the sweet-scented violet flowers of Paulonia. In the South there is the Silver-bell Tree and the deciduous Magnolias, many of which are also to be found in the North.

Wild shrubs which are good autumnal arrangement subjects because of foliage color or berries, or both, include Spicebush, Blueberry, Dogwoods, Bayberry, Highbush-cranberry (*Viburnum triloba*), Sassafras, Snowberry, Virginia Creeper, Red Elderberry, and Winterberry (*Ilex verticillata*). Many of the Viburnums less showy than Highbush-cranberry still bear red or blue berries which hang on quite well, and most of these charming shrubs turn lovely plum red with or before the first frost.

WOODLAND WILD FLOWERS. It pays to grow such wildlings as Jack-in-the-pulpit, Bleeding Hearts, Dutchman's Breeches, Squirrel Corn, and Cyprepediums for judicious use in arrangements. For daintier motifs, try Columbine, Foamflower, Violets, Marsh-marigolds, and woodland Ferns. Skunk Cabbage blooms can be collected freely, and make striking material. Later in the season come the Wood Lily (*Lilium philadelphicum*), the Turk's Cap (*L. superbum*), the Lobelias, including the scarlet Cardinal Flower, and the striking red and white Baneberries. Foliage, flowers, and berries of Clintonia are all beautiful.

IN THE FIELDS, as summer advances, we find Milkweeds, Meadowsweet, Steeplebush, Meadow Rue, Black-eyed Susans, Lupines, Gentians, Queen Anne's Lace, Mallows, and orange Butterfly Weed.

With autumn come Asters, Goldenrods, Joe Pye Weed, Iron Weed, Sunflowers, and Clematis, together with Boneset, False Foxglove, and purple Gerardia.

In making wild-flower arrangements do not become delirious with all the material available. Restrain yourself and be selective. Otherwise you are apt to have a vase of specimens demonstrating how many species you can collect rather than a well-designed arrangement composed of wildlings. The same principles apply to wild-flower arrangements as are followed in other work with cut flowers. As a rule, the simpler the design when using wild material, the more effective. Many artists convert interesting pieces of tree root, bark, or driftwood into containers for such flowers. These seem more appropriate than most other vases or dishes. A metal container for water is secreted somewhere in the heart of the piece of wood. If a conventional container is used, it should be of plain design: a bean pot, pickle jar, earthen pitcher, or low Oriental dish of neutral color and without decoration.

And now another word about conservation before closing this discussion of wildlings. Conservation laws had to be made to save our dwindling natives, and those laws must be obeyed by all. However, if wild material can be taken without damage or loss of plants, from a plot of ground owned by the exhibitor, we cannot see why it should be the duty of any flower-show judge to disqualify an arrangement of wildlings made from such lawfully acquired material. We all know that the conservation laws were made for vandals who sold tons of Holly, Azalea, Laurel, and other wild material for commercial purposes. Unthinking and uneducated individuals also raided the woods and hedgerows, taking more than they could use or keep in good condition. It is ridiculous, however, to believe that one spray of Dogwood or one or two Cypripedium blooms, selected carefully by a flower-arrangement artist from her own grounds, could possibly imperil the country's supply of wild flowers. On the contrary, by displaying this material in a fine arrangement she is teaching others to appreciate the fineness and the beauty of native material.

CHAPTER XXV

Dry and Dormant Material

Those who become interested in the arrangement of dry materials soon find that the possibilities are endless. All that is needed is an observant and perceptive eye and plenty of storage space for the fragile stems, flower heads, seed pods, et cetera. Those without storage space can, of course, discard each arrangement at the end of its usefulness, but it is very handy to have such material on tap. Then, too, things like Lotus pods, Wooden Roses (*Ipomea tuberosa*), and Spoon Cactus are expensive to buy and cannot be too carelessly discarded.

In the Garden

Among *garden flowers* which can be dried and yet retain their color are, first of all, the Everlastings. (These are pleasant in the garden too.) They include Strawflowers (Helichrysums); the Swan River Everlasting (*Rhodanthe manglesi*), daintily colored reddish rose and white; Globe Amaranth; Immortelles (Xeranthemum), white; and Acroclinium. Celosias are familiar to all with their bold plumes of color, and Golden Ageratum (*Lonas inodora*) is much prized by expert arrangers.

Sea-lavender is the most popular form of Statice for dried compositions, but others worth growing for the purpose are *S. sinuata* and *S. suworowi*. Try real lavender also and add fragrance to beauty.

GARDEN FOLIAGE. Gray Artemisias, Oak branches, and Canna foliage are a few suggestions. Experiment as you go by noting in late fall the persistent foliage which, like the Oak leaves, remains after other leaves have disintegrated. Cedar, Juniper, and Yew, with or without berries, are excellent.

SEED PODS are worth studying for dried-material possibilities. One of the finest is the seed pod of the Pawlonia tree. It is often possible to get both this year's and last year's pods, thus giving variety. Catalpa and Locust pods are of interest; and seed heads of Sweet Gum, Tulip Tree, and Sumac. The cones of the various conifers are especially pleasing; and that brings to mind the Gourds, decorative corns, including their husks, and cereal grains which are often combined with them.

Seed pods of many flowers are used; among them, Castor Oil Plant, Oriental Poppies, Monarda, Lunaria or Honesty, Chinese Lanterns, Bittersweet, Globe-thistles, Rose hips, Hydrangeas, and Peonies. For miniatures, try the dainty seed heads of *Alyssum saxatile,* which is rather like Lunaria seen through the wrong end of a telescope.

GRASSES AND BRANCHES. Many lovely grasses are to be found in the garden and by the wayside for filler material, while the branches of Magnolia, Wisteria, Broom, Bittersweet, and Cotinus (Smoke Tree) are desirable for the skeleton or framework lines.

From the Wild

In the autumn, swamps, fields, and hedgerows yield a rich harvest. Cattails are traditional to bring indoors, combined with the plumy heads of swamp grasses. Staghorn Sumac will be found everywhere.

In the fields look for Milkweed pods with their cargo of Kapok-like fluff; Thistles, Mullein; the chestnut-brown seed stalks of Curly Dock (considered invaluable by arrangers of dry material). In the fields, too, you will find Yarrow, Boneset, the little white Pearly Everlastings, Sand Burs, and Teasel. Excellent for silhouette effects.

Go to the meadows or woods for Fern fronds and be sure to get some of the fertile fronds of species like the Ostrich, Cinnamon, and Sensitive Ferns—coarse growers in moist places.

The field grasses include Red Top, Foxtail, Squirreltail, Spike-grass, and the Sedges.

In the hedgerows look for Winterberry, Viburnum fruits, Bittersweet, Spicebush, Hawthorn, Virginia Creeper berries, the gray Bayberry. You may also discover wild Rose hips. But beware of the gray fruits of Poison Ivy, and the hanging gray berries of Poison Sumach.

Either for the skeleton lines of arrangements or as containers for dried material, gnarled tree roots or pieces of silvery driftwood are unexcelled. Keep your eyes open for these gifts of nature when you are in the wild.

And in the woods, collect some of the satiny white or scaly gray fungi which are found on gray Birch and other decaying trees. They can be used for focal interest in dried compositions.

Florists' Material

In the Northeast such material as Southern Magnolia, Eucalyptus, Sandalwood, and Baobab pods are florists' material. Lotus pods, too, are not generally available except by purchase.

Other dried material, which can sometimes be had from florists, are California Pepper berries, Spoon Cactus, Heather, and Wooden Roses—all highly decorative.

For other dried material see Chapter XVI.

Drying Methods

In drying material for arrangements it should be remembered that flowers which are to retain their color must be picked while perfectly fresh, preferably just as they open.

It is convenient to tie Everlasting flowers together in small bunches which can be used as units of color. These can be hung, heads down, in an airy place until ready for use. Strip off the foliage before tying and drying unless you wish to use it as part of the design.

Frail foliage is often better arranged before it is completely dry as there is then less danger of breakage and shattering.

Grasses and grains, like the Everlastings, are fastened together at the stem ends in convenient bunches and should also be hung heads down until used.

Dried branches, especially vines like Wisteria, which take such lovely curves, should be collected when you see a particularly graceful branch or tendril. Keep these in a tall vase, separated so they will not become entangled, until ready for use.

Delicate Fern fronds are sometimes pressed and kept flat until needed.

Seed pods can be stored in suit boxes between layers of shelf paper or in smaller boxes in a cupboard drawer.

CHAPTER XXVI

Arrangements Around the Year

Each season brings its quota of flowers which are particularly desirable for indoor decoration. It is helpful to the arranger to know at a glance what is or could be available in any particular month.

First of all, there are the florists' flowers which she can buy. Better transportation has made it possible for florists to offer certain items like Snapdragons and Gladiolus every month in the year. In the winter they come from the South. In summer they are grown in the North. Other cut flowers are strictly seasonal, like forced spring-flowering bulbs. By consulting the lists in this chapter you can ascertain in a moment just what flowers can be purchased in any month. In this way it will be possible for you to plan your arrangement before purchasing flowers, since you know in advance what is in the market.

In the same way, a study of the lists of garden and window garden plants will tell you what you have, or can grow if you wish, to keep up a constant supply of flowers and foliage for arrangements throughout the year.

Those of us who are fortunate enough to have gardens can save materially by planning and planting to provide flowers for cutting through a long season. These may be supplemented by foliage, berries, and such plants as Witchhazel and Hellebore in winter.

It is not enough for the enthusiastic arranger to have a garden of profuse bloom. To be really efficient she should plan and plant with arrangements especially in mind. Many lovely garden flowers are not ideal for cutting. Among these are fleeting blooms like Day-lilies and those which close at night like Evening Primrose. Study the monthly lists and plan to plant accordingly. Make yours an arranger's garden.

Still another rich source of flower-arrangement material may be found among house plants. It is fun to visit local greenhouses and to look up growers who offer unusual items. Then, too, there are the tender winter-flowering bulbs which can be purchased at the same time as the hardy bulbs, planted in pots, and brought to winter bloom for use in arrangements. A few blooms, purchased or produced in the window garden, can be supplemented by the showy foliage of Begonias, Dracaenas, Dieffenbachias, et cetera. I keep one Spotted Begonia plant in a large pot especially for use in winter arrangements. The beautiful foliage with rose-color reverse sides and silver spots on top goes well with any number of flowers. In addition, the plant produces showy clusters of large rose-pink blooms. Many women who arrange flowers frequently keep such plants in reserve for supplementary material. Though the symmetry of such specimens may be destroyed by cutting so that they have to be kept like Cinderellas in a kitchen window or other out-of-the-way corner, they are nonetheless rewarding in the work they do toward beautifying the home.

It will pay you then to consult the following lists carefully and to keep them always available for ready reference.

January

FROM THE FLORIST
Cut Flowers

Acacia
Agapanthus
Amaryllis
Anemone
Anthurium
Antirrhinum
Begonias
Bouvardia
Buddleia
Calanthe
Calendula
Calla-lily
Camellia
Carnation
Cornflower
Daffodils
Delphinium

Euphorbia
Freesia
Gardenia
Gerbera
Gladiolus
Gloriosa-lily
Heather
Iris, Bulbous
Lilac
Lilies:
    Album
    Auratum
    Longiflorum
    Speciosum rubrum
Lily-of-the-valley
Muscari

Nerine
Orchids:
    Cattleya
    Cyprepedium
    Oncidium
    Phalaenopsis
    Vanda
Pansies
Poppies
Primulas
Pyrethrum
Ranunculus
Roses
Strelitzia
Sweet Peas
Tulips
Violets

Plants

Azaleas
Cyclamen
Daffodils
Fuchsias

Gardenia
Geraniums

Hyacinth
Kalanchoe
Marguerite
Primulas

FROM THE GARDEN

Evergreens, broad-leaf   Evergreens, coniferous

FROM THE WINDOW GARDEN

Amaryllis
Begonias, winter-blooming
Calla-lily   Freesia

Kalanchoe
Veltheimia
Foliage plants

Arrangement by Mrs. A. E. Luedy. Courtesy Cleveland Garden Center

JANUARY: Christmas Roses (Helleborus) and Witchhazel. They both really bloom in the snow!

February

FROM THE FLORIST
Cut Flowers

Acacia
Amaryllis
Anemone
Anthurium
Antirrhinum
Arbutus
Bouvardia
Buddleia
Calendula
Calla-lily
Camellia
Carnation
Cornflower
Daffodils
Euphorbia

Freesia
Gardenia
Gerbera
Gladiolus
Gloriosa-lily
Heather
Iris, Bulbous
Lace-flower
Lilac
Lilies, various
Lily-of-the-valley
Mignonette
Montbretias

Muscari
Nerine
Orchids, various
Pansies
Poppies
Primulas
Pyrethrum
Ranunculus
Roses
Stephanotis
Stocks
Strelitzia
Sweet Peas
Tulips
Violets

Plants

Begonias
Calceolarias
Cinerarias
Cyclamen

Daffodils
Fuchsias
Gardenia
Hyacinth

Marguerite
Primulas
Tulips

Arrangement by Mrs. Bertram Flory, Jr.

*FEBRUARY: A few florists' flowers—Stocks,
Roses, Freesias, and Ranunculus.*

March

FROM THE FLORIST
Cut Flowers

Acacia
Agapanthus
Amaryllis
Anemone
Arbutus
Calendula
Calla-lily
Camellia
Carnation
Cornflower
Daphne
Freesia
Gerbera

Gladiolus
Gloriosa-lily
Heather
Iris, Bulbous
Lilac
Lilies, various
Lily-of-the-valley
Mignonette
Montbretias
Muscari
Orchids, various

Pansies
Poppies
Primulas
Pyrethrum
Ranunculus
Roses
Scabiosa
Stephanotis
Stocks
Strelitzia
Sweet Peas
Tulips
Violets

Plants

Astilbes
Begonias
Cyclamen
Daffodils

Fuchsias
Geraniums
Hyacinth

Hydrangeas
Lilies, Easter
Roses
Tulips

FROM THE GARDEN

Crocuses
Flowering shrub branches (forced)
Flowering fruit branches (forced)

Pussywillows
Snowdrops
Spring-flowering Bulbs

MARCH: From the window garden—Geraniums with their own foliage.

April

FROM THE FLORIST
Cut Flowers

Amaryllis	Freesia	Muscari
Anemone	Gardenia	Nasturtiums
Anthurium	Gerbera	Orchids, various
Antirrhinum	Gladiolus	Pansies
Arbutus	Gloriosa-lily	Primulas
Calendula	Gypsophila	Roses
Calla-lily	Iris, Bulbous	Scabiosa
Carnation	Lilac	Stephanotis
Cornflower	Lilies, various	Stocks
Daffodils	Lupin	Strelitzia
Daphne	Mignonette	Tulips
Delphinium	Montbretias	Violets

Plants

Astilbes		Hydrangeas
Begonias	Geraniums	Lilies, Easter
Daffodils	Heliotrope	Roses
Fuchsias	Hyacinth	Tulips

FROM THE GARDEN

Azaleas	Leucothoe	Shrubs, flowering
Chionodoxas	Magnolias	Squills
Crocuses	Muscari	Trollius
Daffodils	Primulas	Tulips (species and
Fritillarias	Scillas	species hybrids)

Arrangement by Mrs. Willard Schneider

APRIL: *Spring at last—with Trumpet Daffodils, Forsythia and Pussy willows.*

May

FROM THE FLORIST

Cut Flowers

Anemone	Gardenia	Orchids, various
Anthurium	Gerbera	Pansies
Antirrhinums	Gladiolus	Peony
Aquilegia	Gloriosa-lily	Primulas
Bouvardia	Iris, Bulbous	Roses
Buddleia	Lilac	Scabiosa
Calendula	Lilies, various	Stephanotis
Calla-lily	Lily-of-the-valley	Stocks
Carnation	Lupin	Sweet Peas
Cornflower	Mignonette	Tulips
Daffodils	Montbretias	Violets
Delphinium	Muscari	Waterlily
Freesia	Nasturtiums	Zinnia

Plants

Begonias		Geraniums
Fuchsias	Heliotrope	Hyacinth

FROM THE GARDEN

Aquilegia	Myosotis
Azaleas	Pansies
Dianthus	Peonies
Dicentra	*Phlox divaricata*
Digitalis	Rhododendron
Doronicum	Shrubs, flowering
Gaillardia	Statice
Geum	Trollius
Heuchera	Tulips
Iris	Violas
Kalmia	Violets
Lily-of-the-valley	Wisteria

Arrangement by Mrs. Robert Straub

MAY: Tulips informally arranged to counteract their usual stiffness.

June

FROM THE FLORIST
Cut Flowers

Anthurium		Pansies
Antirrhinum	Gerbera	Peony
Aquilegia	Gladiolus	Primulas
Asters, China	Gloriosa-lily	Pyrethrum
Bouvardia	Gypsophila	Ranunculus
Buddleia	Larkspur	Roses
Calendula	Lilies, various	Scabiosa
Calla-lily	Lily-of-the-valley	Shasta Daisy
Carnation	Lupin	Stocks
Cornflower	Marguerite	Sweet Peas
Dahlia	Marigolds	Tritoma
Delphinium	Mignonette	Tuberose
Gaillardia	Nasturtiums	Waterlily
Gardenia	Orchids, various	Zinnia

Plants

Begonias	Fuchsias	Geraniums

FROM THE GARDEN

Alliums		Peonies
Antirrhinum	Gaillardia	Poppies
Astilbes	Heuchera	Pyrethrum
Campanulas	Iris	Rhododendron
Coreopsis	Kalmia	Roses
Delphinium	Lily, Madonna	Rudbeckia
Dianthus	Lupin	Scabiosa
Digitalis	Myosotis	Sweet Peas
Dimorphotheca	Penstemons	Yucca

Arrangement by Mrs. Claire Stickles

JUNE: Roses, indoors as well as out.

July

FROM THE FLORIST
Cut Flowers

Agapanthus	Eucharis	Mignonette
Alstroemeria	Gardenia	Pansies
Anthurium	Gerbera	Primulas
Antirrhinum	Gladiolus	Pyrethrum
Aquilegia	Gloriosa-lily	Ranunculus
Asters, China	Gypsophila	Roses
Bouvardia	Iris, Japanese	Scabiosa
Carnation	Larkspur	Shasta Daisy
Clivia	Liatris	Stocks
Cornflower	Lilies, various	Sweet Peas
Dahlia	Lily-of-the-valley	Tritoma
Delphinium	Marguerite	Tuberose

Plants

Begonias	Fuchsias	Geraniums

FROM THE GARDEN

Abelia	Echinops	Platycodon
Aconitum	Fuchsias	Poppies
Anthemis	Gaillardia	Roses
Arctotis	Geraniums	*Salvia farinacea*
Butterfly Weed	Geum	Salpiglossis
Campanulas	Gladiolus	Santolina
Centaureas	Gypsophila	Scabiosa
Clematis	Iris, Japanese	Shasta Daisies
Coreopsis	Ismenes	Sweet Peas, annual
Dahlia	Lilies	Sweet Peas, perennial
Delphinium	Marigolds	Tritoma
Dianthus	Nasturtiums	Verbena
Digitalis	Petunias	Violas
Dimorphotheca	Phloxes	Zinnia

JULY'S Marigolds go well in containers of copper or brass.

August

FROM THE FLORIST
Cut Flowers

Agapanthus		Marguerite
Alstroemeria	Gaillardia	Marigolds
Anthurium	Gardenia	Mignonette
Antirrhinum	Gerbera	Nasturtiums
Asters, China	Gladiolus	Nigella
Celosia	Gloriosa-lily	Pyrethrum
Chrysanthemums	Gypsophila	Roses
Clivia	Larkspur	Scabiosa
Cornflower	Liatris	Shasta Daisy
Dahlia	Lilies, various	Tritoma
Delphinium	Lily-of-the-valley	Tuberose
Eucharis		Zinnia

Plants

Begonias	Geraniums

FROM THE GARDEN

Anthemis	Goldenrods	Nasturtiums
Antirrhinum	Heliotrope	Onion blossoms
Asters, China	Hostas	Petunias
Begonia, Tuberous	Lace-flower	Phlox, Garden
Calendula	Lantana	Roses
Campanulas	Larkspur	Rudbeckias
Celosia	Leek blossoms	Salpiglossis
Centaureas	Liatris	Salvias
Cosmos	Lilies	Stocks
Dahlias	Lupin	Stokesias
Delphiniums	Lycoris	Tritoma
Echinops	Marigolds	Santolina
Geraniums	Moonflower	Sunflowers
Gladiolus	Montbretia	Verbena
Globe Artichoke	Mignonette	Zinnia

AUGUST: In hot weather, simple arrangements appeal. Zinnias are easy.

September

FROM THE FLORIST
Cut Flowers

Agapanthus	Delphinium	Marigolds
Alstroemeria	Gardenia	Physalis
Anthurium	Gerbera	Roses
Antirrhinum	Gladiolus	Scabiosa
Aster, China	Gloriosa-lily	Shasta Daisy
Celosia	Larkspur	Strelitzia
Chrysanthemums	Liatris	Tritoma
Cornflower	Lilies, various	Tuberose
Dahlia	Lily-of-the-valley	Zinnia

Plants

Begonias		Geraniums
Chrysanthemums	Gardenia	Shrimp Plant

FROM THE GARDEN

Aconitum	Clematis	Marigolds
Anemones,	*Cobaea scandens*	Moonflower
Japanese	Cosmos	Myosotis
Antirrhinum	Dahlia	Nasturtiums
Artemesia	Delphinium	Petunias
Asters, China	Dianthus	Salvias
Asters, hardy	Eupatorium	Santolina
Calendulas	Gaillardia	Shrubs, berried
Campanulas	Gladiolus	Sunflowers
Catananche	Globe Artichoke	Verbena
Celosia	Goldenrods	Violas
Chrysanthemums	Lilies	Zinnia

Arrangement by Mrs. Innis Brown

SEPTEMBER *fruits and vegetables occasionally take the place of flowers, especially for the dining table.*

October

FROM THE FLORIST
Cut Flowers

Antirrhinum		Orchids, various
Bouvardia	Gardenia	Physalis
Calla-lily	Gerbera	Roses
Carnation	Gladiolus	Stephanotis
Chrysanthemums	Gloriosa-lily	Strelitzia
Cornflower	Liatris	Tritoma
Dahlia	Lilies, various	Tuberose
Delphinium	Lily-of-the-valley	Zinnia

Plants

Chrysanthemums	Geraniums
Gardenias	Shrimp Plant

FROM THE GARDEN

Asters, China		Marigolds
Asters, hardy	*Cobaea scandens*	Petunias
Calendulas	Colchicums	Roses
Chrysanthemums	Cosmos	Shrubs, berried
Clematis	Eupatorium	Zinnia

Arrangement by Mrs. Stanley J. Chute

OCTOBER: Autumnal colors, from woods, fields, and the late garden, suggest the fading year. A good season for monochrome arrangements— though you won't find Freesias, even at the florist's.

November

FROM THE FLORIST
Cut Flowers

Anemone	Euphorbia	Physalis
Anthurium	Gardenia	Primulas
Antirrhinum	Gerbera	Pyrethrum
Asters, China	Gladiolus	Ranunculus
Bouvardia	Godetia	Roses
Calla-lily	Heather	Stephanotis
Camellia	Lilies, various	Strelitzia
Carnation	Lily-of-the-valley	Sweet Peas
Chrysanthemums	Nerine	Tritoma
Cornflower	Orchids, various	Tuberose

Plants

Azaleas		Gardenia
Chrysanthemums	Cyclamen	Geraniums

FROM THE GARDEN

Chrysanthemums	Shrubs, berried	Witchhazel

Arrangement by Mrs. Claire Stickles

NOVEMBER: Flinging a final defiance in Jack Frost's teeth, the hardy Mums brighten outdoor gardens and glorify indoor rooms.

December

FROM THE FLORIST
Cut Flowers

Acacia
Anemone
Anthurium
Antirrhinum
Asters, China
Begonias
Bouvardia
Buddleia
Calla-lily
Camellia
Carnation
Chrysanthemums

Cornflower
Daffodils
Delphinium
Euphorbia
Freesia
Gardenia
Gerbera
Gladiolus
Gloriosa-lily
Heather

Lilies, various
Lily-of-the-valley
Nerine
Orchids, various
Pansies
Poppies
Pyrethrum
Ranunculus
Roses
Strelitzia
Sweet Peas
Violets

Plants

Azaleas
Begonia, Christmas
Cyclamen
Decorative Pepper

Fuchsias
Gardenia

Jerusalem Cherry
Kalanchoe
Poinsettia
Primulas

FROM THE GARDEN
Hellebore

FROM THE WINDOW GARDEN

Christmas Cactus
Poinsettia

Cyclamen
Decorative Pepper

Jerusalem Cherry
Kalanchoe

Arrangement by Mrs. Lillian Norstad

DECEMBER: *And florists' flowers again take over and carry on, while we dream and plan for still better arrangements in the year to come.*

Index

299

Index

Index

Index

Index

Index